Earth's Elders

EARTH'S ELDERS

EARTH'S ELDERS

The Wisdom of the World's Oldest People

Words and photographs by Jerry Friedman

with Essays by
Robert Coles, Lama Surya Das, Dr. M. Joycelyn Elders,
and Arvol Looking Horse

Edited by Mark Chimsky-Lustig

For information please address:

Earth's Elders Foundation, Inc.
PO Box 111
South Kent, CT 06785

Book design by Leah Carlson-Stanisic
Cover design by Lynn Landry

ISBN: 0-9769108-0-2

Orders, inquiries, and correspondence should be addressed to:

Earth's Elders Foundation, Inc.
PO Box 111
South Kent, CT 06785
(860) 354-3494 FAX (860) 354-9667

Printed in Canada

10 9 8 7 6 5 4 3 2 1

In gratitude, to my mother and father, grandparents,
and the generations before them
and to Watty Piper, who showed me the way

ACKNOWLEDGMENTS

OVER THE COURSE OF THIS JOURNEY, I have made every attempt to verify the ages, the accounts, and the historical anecdotes that make up the biographical sketches in this book. Most of the names of the supercentenarians have come from one primary source, Robert Young, without whom this project could not have been completed. A few I found on my own. We are all, however, dependent upon, and are subject to the veracity of others when it comes to establishing the accounts and the exact ages of the supercentenarians in this book.

From beginning to end, I have relied upon a host of people to point me in the right direction and help me along the way. I am deeply grateful to all. Many thanks to my translators, arrangers, and guides: to Baba in Japan, to Hari in Holland, to Juan Pretus in Spain, Filipe Prista Lucas in Portugal, Ochir Tsogtbileg and his family in Mongolia.

To my friends who have endured countless hours of coffee shop discussions, I thank you for all your suggestions and constructive criticisms. To Hironobu Shindo, Guli Arshad, Adam Paton, Shikhar Ghosh, Bob Schmidt, Helen Hamlin, and Jean-Paul Gimon who encouraged and gave me counsel. To the essayists, Bob Coles, Lama

Surya Das, Dr. Elders, and Arvol Looking Horse for their help. To Stephen Michaels, Mark Harris, and Rinaldo Frattolillo for their thoughtful support and literary criticism.

To Zach and Zoë, who gave me inspiration and help, and to Cheryl, who put up with my long trips away and longer days and nights of writing. To Ann and Emily Strem for their editing skills. To the guys at the studio, Satoshi and Carl, to Dan Lipow who engineered the images through a digital maze and helped create the photo exhibitions based on this book.

To Dr. Eric Bates for his patience in explaining molecular biology to a layman. To Tod Seisser and Stephanie Arnold, for their visual and intellectual input, and their humor. To Dickon Pownall-Gray and David Wilk who offered publishing opportunities and a special thanks to my editor, Mark Chimsky-Lustig, for his tireless work on this project.

Table of Contents

Part Three: The Elders 73

We are who they were,
and they are who we will be . . .

"WHAT IN THE WORLD AM I DOING?" My hands were numb and my feet, submerged under the deep snow, had absolutely no feeling. The ancient furry pony I was riding trudged up the treeless landscape to the top of the hill where in every direction I saw only white except for the gray-purple shadows of distant mountains fifty miles away. "I must be out of my mind," I thought. "The steppes of Mongolia. The dead of winter. Forty degrees below zero."

This journey started as an innocent idea, or so I'd thought. How could I have known then where it was going to lead? One morning I drove from Connecticut to Boston to view a sculpture show of a retired Princeton physicist. I was escorted by my ninety-year-old mother, whom I frequently visited, as we wandered around the wood-and-string sculptures conceived and built by another ninety-year-old resident of my mother's care facility. The response from those who lived there was wonderful and it made me think of how many places around the country had similar residents full of talent and energy who didn't have the opportunity to share them with others, except for those who lived there or the occasional visitor. Many residents are isolated from the public, placed there by family members or by self-imposed exile, living out their years as part of a satellite subculture.

As an experiment, I decided to spend four days at my mother's care facility to try to imagine my elder years. A few days later, having immersed myself in this home and felt firsthand the rhythm of this life, it struck me—wouldn't it be fascinating to photograph some of the older or oldest residents and create an exhibition of their portraits and biographies that could travel to similar communities of elders? Having been a professional advertising photographer in New York City my whole working life, I realized that I could use the tools of my trade to contribute to something meaningful. I began my exploration with a small group. My mother's friend Lottie, the oldest resident at 102, was also one of the happiest and healthiest of the group, with clear recollections of her long life. One smile from this tiny, stooped woman was like rays of sun breaking around a storm cloud. I was hooked. What I learned from her, and ultimately from a diverse group of "supercentenarians" (those elders 110 years old and up), resulted in simple recurring truths about all of us and, in particular, those who have lived the longest.

Fate has played a strong hand in the last few years. By chance and good fortune, a simple email landed me in Atlanta where I began a wonderful collaboration with demographer Robert Young, a senior sleuth of the Gerontology Research Group. His data bank gave me compass and direction for my search. I was given a rare opportunity to benefit from years' worth of his research and, figuratively, he became a companion along the journey. Robert maintained an extensive database of pending and validated supercentenarians from around the world that proved invaluable. His work, to sort through and cross-reference birth certificates, census records, and family Bibles, provided names based on three authenticated documents. The caveat in some "cases" was that all the cross-checking and exhaustive research was not complete but that the evidence seemed to point toward validated ages. As Robert wrote to me early on, "There is no scientifically valid method for accurately assessing the age of an adult-aged individual. The only way to ascertain a person's age, then, is through the written record. For millennia, claims of people living to age 110 and greater have abounded; however, no serious system of national recordkeeping, recording the vital statistics of an entire population (as opposed to just the royalty first and then nobility) came into existence until 1749, when Sweden became the first nation in the world to attempt such a feat. Even then, it would take about a hundred years to get the system reliable enough that the data could be relied upon, at least for extreme ages at the upper end of the scale. Centralized birth registration began in the U.K. in 1837, and in the U.S. only in 1933. For some poorer nations, adequate systems of record-keeping for the population still are not in place." For Africa, South America, even China, this was a significant obstacle for me.

After researching the plausibility of taking the portraits of the oldest people in America, I set on a course of discovery that ultimately took me not only across the United States but also around the world. Along the way, people tried to dissuade me from attempting this personal assignment. What was I going to accomplish? What was the point? What credentials did I have? Why would I attempt to finance this out of my own pocket, without a paying assignment, or at least without being reimbursed at the end? Others before me had given up at the early stages, after losing the trail. Well, I was a successful photographer; I had had a career in advertising, having had the top corporations in the world as clients; I had been given financial comfort; and I had an instinctual need to somehow give back after years of taking from the system.

Shortly after beginning the project, I was introduced through a friend to a *National Geographic* photographer who had made a similar attempt over the years. I wanted to talk with him about the obstacles I might face. One morning over coffee, with my first few images spread out in a diner booth, he talked about his experiences finding supercentenarians while he was between professional assignments, tracking down people whom he had heard were very old. Some were truly old, many were not, and many he never found. "I've spent twenty years in and out of this personal project, trying to devote time between assignments like I did in Russia," he said. "Someday I'll go back to it." He abandoned the project but kept the idea for future resurrection. I was sobered but not discouraged by his candor. He liked my images. He wished me luck.

At the core of my thinking was a willingness to be open, to have no predetermined plan of where I was going. I began my journey by locating as many of the oldest people on earth as I could find. Each supercentenarian was 110 years old or older, and each had his or her own unique story, spanning more than a century of history, having actually lived through three centuries.

One was more intriguing than the next. Initially, almost every time I'd arrive in a new place, exhausted from hours of traveling and squinting at marked-up maps, the same question would resurface. "What am I doing this for?" I'd look around and think, "I'm in a different country, or at the very least a different culture. I could be sitting comfortably at home." On my quest to find as many supercentenarians as I could, I've spent a night in an old castle in Scotland. I've traveled to a small island off the coast of Spain. I've found myself in a barren village in Portugal. I've stayed in a Soviet-built mausoleum in Ulaanbaatar. I've driven through the prairie of the Midwest and the backwoods of Kentucky. I've been jetlagged in Okinawa and spent a frosty evening in Amsterdam on my way to a village near Germany. I've dined at a strip mall in Virginia, and ferried across the Chesapeake. I've spent a sleepless night upstairs from a noisy pub near Liverpool and slept by the side of the road in Nebraska. At fifty-five, I wasn't a kid anymore, and the challenges were sometimes daunting.

So why did I persevere? I began to recognize the seeds of discovery after the second portrait. I took notes at each interview and reread them in my motel room at night. I tried to picture the supercentenarians I met as young people in a different time. I looked at the Polaroids, at the faces of the day. My own viewpoint about the elderly went through a slow but dramatic transformation. After a while, I began to organize my amateur observations into categories. Common threads in the elders' stories began to form a structure that explained their longevity. That's when the project began to get exciting. It didn't matter if the supercentenarians were from Georgia or Japan. Boundaries didn't matter, nor did their skin or their speech. What did matter was that I was documenting their stories, their faith, their attitudes, and those of the seniors around them who were invisible and whose voices were being forgotten by history. In the biographies, you will learn for yourself what has helped them to reach the outer edge of human longevity. Ultimately, what I learned was not just to hear them, but to truly listen to what they had to say.

A smile in Hiroshima; a chuckle in the Allegheny Mountains. A hand squeeze in Yokohama; a cry for help in East Boston. I was developing an extended family. I realized that while I should have been as dispassionate as a typical reporter, I was caring more and more about these people, how they were feeling, how they would get along after I left. I still try to stay in touch with many of them today.

There have been days, as I sat in front of my laptop reviewing my notes or tapes of the interviews, when I would pause, rummage through the files for a number, and pick up the phone. One morning the call was to the daughter of 111-year-old Doris Prater in Warwickshire, England.

"Hello, Mrs. Daniels, this is Jerry Friedman in the U.S. How've you been? How's your mother?"

"She's not doing too well. She's had a bad spell the last few weeks," she replied.

"Mrs. Daniels," I said, "I'm sending you a flier from my photography show in Japan. Your mother was chosen as the poster girl for the show. Her face was all over Tokyo."

"Get on, was she now? Oh my, Mum will be so pleased when I tell her. Thank you so much for calling."

When I hung up I was beaming. I could picture Mrs. Daniels in her parlor in the little town of Rugby, Warwickshire, delightedly informing her "Mum" of her new-found fame. Doris would nod, taking in the happy news that she was now a celebrated supercentenarian, and then go back to dozing in her rocking chair by the heater.

Not all the experiences were filled with such delight. Some were unsettling, others surreal. Once, on a cold crisp Saturday morning, I sat in my rental car in the deserted parking lot of an elder care facility in rural Indiana, waiting to meet a 110-year-old woman. The night before, I had been the only inhabitant of a powder-blue motel with dangling shutters on the outskirts of town. I had heard my travel mantra in my head again: "Where am I and what am I doing?" I felt the same as I had in Mongolia. But by now I was driven by the chance to meet another new, wonderfully special person. My whole concept of aging had noticeably changed. As I waited in the car, sipping my coffee, a white van pulled up. A woman in a trench coat got out and opened the back bay doors. She entered the retirement home by a wide door next to the entrance that seemed to blend into the wall. She reappeared pushing a gurney with a body bag. The body was conveyed into the back of the van. The trench-coated lady closed the doors and drove away. I had the sinking feeling that the woman I had come to photograph was in the body bag.

In this case, my feeling was wrong. Nevertheless, I was haunted by a poignant image of two doors standing side by side, one the entrance of the care facility and the other, the exit. One for the living, one for the dead. I eventually did meet my 110-year-old subject and added her amazing story to my collection. However, the images of that day served as a persistent reminder of the frailty of life and fueled my sense of urgency about the power and purpose of this project.

When did I recognize the significance of what I was doing or, more to the point, of how this project was changing me? I can't point to one moment when a shift occurred, but change began with a word: notice. I didn't hear voices, but I heard the word in my head. I hadn't noticed the elderly before this project nor had I noticed my thoughts about them. There was no cause to analyze, nor I suppose would there have been a need to had I not begun this project. It took emotional time for me to think this out, to consider my beliefs, and to be honest about my true feelings about what I was doing and what this was doing to me. From the first supercentenarian I photographed to the last one I've just met, I have been remade, both figuratively and practically, each time. In *The Adventures of Huckleberry Finn*, one of my favorite books, Twain depicted Huck's education and the development of his character through a series of adventures along the Mississippi. I thought about Huck, and me, as I crossed the same river on my way past Hannibal a few weeks ago. I have always thought Mark Twain was a master at provoking thought through Huck's adventures, painting pictures with prose that addressed a range of social issues of his day. Any parallel ended at the river.

In the beginning, the very first portrait put me on notice. I was not prepared. I had come from a discipline of being in control in a studio, producing images with a staff supported by enormous amounts of equipment. Always working on a schedule, dictating the pace, and in some cases even the angle of a pose, I produced images based on my arrangement of objects. After twenty years, I closed my studio, sold my equipment, and retired at a pretty young age. So here I was starting all over again: renting a carload of equipment and hiring an assistant. I approached this as a tryout, an "experiment," before committing fully to the idea.

I was made to wait one hour while the first supercentenarian, Mrs. Smith, finished her dessert. And because I had yet to develop any kind of rapport with someone who was that old, quite honestly she made me uncomfortable. Her age was actually an impediment. She decided she didn't want to answer many of my questions and stopped talking to me. She was testing me. At 112, time was of no importance to her. I realized for the first time that I was dealing with an entirely different model category. It was her will against mine and she dictated the terms. And then I had the first inkling of what was to be a long process of re-examination. I was about to learn how to view the inside, not just the outside, of someone. What was time? What mattered? A schedule, a deadline, or waiting patiently? She deserved my deference. What she knew was worth the wait. My re-education had begun.

And then the second portrait, a magical moment, proved to me how special supercentenarians were. What I learned from this man was more than historical information, though there were fascinating and humorous stories. Fred Hale, Sr., made me laugh, he made me visualize his past, and he made me wish for more of his knowledge. There was almost an air of mystery that surrounded his life story. Hackneyed as it may sound, I began to learn about myself through this man. I repacked my thinking, my equipment; decided I couldn't afford an assistant going forward, so I set out solo on the trail.

And then the third, the fourth, the fifth portrait, and the momentum overtook me. These people and their stories captivated me. It didn't matter to me that I felt somewhat isolated from friends or family. I know they thought I had "lost my grip." There was no financial benefit to this work, no visible payday. Maybe I had begun to see a bigger picture and they hadn't.

No matter, I was on my way.

As it happened, the direction changed my first year. I was in Georgia when it first hit me, and then again in Maryland. There was a back-story surrounding every portrait: that of all the elderly people around me who suffered in silence. I began to realize that I was taking portraits of people who could very well help those whose portraits I would never take. So, I mulled it over, talked with others, and shared my thoughts. The idea of traveling exhibitions of these portraits took on an even greater importance to me, and soon I confirmed the payoff to myself. All this unexposed knowledge could be a vehicle to tap into people's deepest emotions and inspire them to do something, to help a group that had become isolated and marginalized. I was beginning to digest my feelings about the elderly. I hadn't quite been reinvented; I was still harboring many age prejudices that accompany my generation.

So, I kept going. Robert Young had become my guide for the venture. We traded information and we kept in contact as I traveled around the world. After one of the last trips, which again came from Robert's information, he wrote me to ask, "What did you think of the family?" To which I wrote back, "I considered this to have been one of the more exceptional experiences I've had along the way." He responded, "Yes, going to meet that family was like that television program *Touched by an Angel*. The family was so unique." I sensed that Robert had shifted his view of me from his early skepticism to considering me a credible colleague.

I became an explorer, from Treasure Island to Es Migjorn Gran. I became the leading expert on supercentenarians, not by design, but by default. No one else in history has ever met so many of the oldest people on earth. I became a guide or scout for a gerontologist and geneticist from Harvard Medical School, providing names and possible research information for the first genetic study of supercentenarians ever made. I had coffee with an evolutionary biologist in Barcelona. I've corresponded with doctors in Beijing. I've given an impromptu talk to a group of captains of industry at a hunting lodge in the Colorado Rockies. Over and over, the encounters remade me, forcing me to learn about a subject in so many different ways. As I spoke with experts on the many different aspects of aging, supercentenarians made me take on this mantle, so to speak, very seriously. It was out of the spontaneous Colorado presentation that the way changed again, and a nonprofit educational foundation, Earth's Elders Foundation, was conceived and formed. In the process, I changed from a passive photographer to a pro-active biographer.

The birth of the foundation was pastoral. The day after my talk in the Colorado bunkhouse, two men walked with me through the woods and reviewed and critiqued my speech from the night before. By the time we reached the tree line, they had recognized not only what had been accomplished but also what still needed to be done to fulfill the larger goals of the mission. A nonprofit educational foundation was needed to raise the awareness of the public and develop empathy in children toward the plight of the elderly. It was a construct that public and private institutions understood, and these men would assist in its construction. Formalizing my ideas within an educational foundation would help move my ambition from a personal, emotional desire to a concrete success. This book was a logical goal and a building block of the mission. As of this writing, the foundation is developing teaching programs for the young, based on the lives of the supercentenarians, to address issues of aging in our culture. Hopefully Earth's Elders Foundation will nurture others to take a chance and explore themselves and their attitudes toward aging. Photographic shows are being scheduled for schools and public spaces around the world. I've been asked to speak to the public about my work. I am speaking at the UN where the foundation will have a show. Four years have flown by.

Tied to each portrait in this book was a life story that gave me a little more clarity about the issues surrounding aging. Tied to each insight was the awareness that these aged souls were transforming me. I have been nudged by this new self-awareness to make a small difference in other people's lives. As a photographer, the metaphor of the camera seemed most appropriate for my change in vision. There are times when a macro lens is suitable, but you also need to understand when a wide-angle lens is the best choice to broaden the scope of understanding or convey an idea. One lens, one vision does not work in all situations.

Somewhere along the way, maybe while lying on a bed gazing at a motel ceiling, I recalled one of my earliest encounters with an elderly person. I was a little boy of maybe three, sitting on my grandmother's lap in her living room. It was a Sunday morning ritual for my father to take me with him to visit his mother. What I remember most was her warm breath on my face, a smell that was different and older than my mother's, her sweet elderly perfume, and the mushy wet kisses that she left on my cheek as she hugged and squeezed me. I knew she was old; her skin didn't look like mine, and she was always sitting in a chair. There was a certain awkwardness on my part, an awareness of the difference between us that was evident even way back then. I felt uncomfortable. Even at that young age, I was setting my feet on a path of distancing myself from the elderly. No one set me straight.

Memories of my childhood, however, are also filled with fables and family stories from the oldest generation who passed on their history for me, forming an early template for my understanding of the world around me. In my family's stories of coming to America were certain core themes of right and wrong, of moral and ethical conduct, that went beyond the culture of any age. One grandfather, Samuel Friedman, fled the pogroms of Latvia to the United States and the other, Jacob Kahan, a source of endless stories and inspiration, was undoubtedly the only Jewish–Native American medicine man in the South. Grandpa's picture was created in my mind through our family stories of a six-foot-tall Indian medicine man with jet-black hair, a feathered headdress, and buckskin jacket, putting up his teepee on the edge of town. Other memories, passed down to me remain with me still: my mother's and grandmother's embarrassment as they would come into town on a buckboard with my mother banging a drum; the elixir Grandpa Nanzetta (he had bought a new name for an additional disguise) would sell to cure all ills; his elaborate cover-up to avoid being detected as a Jew in the rural South. I have a story-picture of my other grandfather rummaging through a mountain of old discarded leather shoes to make a pair to sell in his shop, or his sending for a stranger from his former shtetl to be his bride. They embraced the American dream; they lived its opportunities and disappointments. Their narratives were my conduits to an earlier generation and a past that sparked my boundless imagination. I listened to their memories passed down to me and saw them as action stories of relatives running the gauntlet of life, enduring and sometimes succeeding. Now I know them in a different context; now I'm ready to listen to the deeper meaning of the lives they led.

I confess to past hypocrisy. The very prejudice that I see around me, that I'm working to change in others, I didn't acknowledge in myself for a very long time. These biases were obviously planted in my youth. Who am I to preach to others? At best, I can erect a signpost that people can see. I am a product of a society that teaches us that aging is a desperate fate. We are taught to celebrate the magic of childbirth, to marvel at the early years of growth, to delight in the joy of watching a child develop. But all these positive descriptions of the stages of growth seem to fade after a while as new stages take their place, and we are left with a sense that maturity merely signals failing youth, and that to grow old is to become irrelevant. The underlying assumption is that health and vitality also disappear when we age.

The overarching conclusion that I have come to after traveling around the world on this project is that these assumptions are false. Vitality and health are not the exclusive domains of youth, nor is relevancy. The old should be venerated. There is so much to learn if we are willing to listen. The inspirational supercentenarians profiled in this book are the poster people for longevity. They have shared their thoughts and life wisdom with me. They comprise one of the rarest and most scientifically fascinating groups in the world. As I explored their stories, I felt inspired to discover more about the common denominators and secrets to longevity that united them. From the moment of birth, we begin the process of aging, obvious but rarely recognized, and whether on a daily basis or as we make specific passages from one stage to another, we all grapple with the aging process and look for answers. If you connect with the portraits in the book and listen closely to their lives, you may find your own answers to leading a life that is not just long, but fulfilling as well.

I thought it appropriate to ask others to help me craft a fuller picture of the important issues that surround aging in our culture and that need to be addressed now. Their collective expertise grounds this book and gives it strength. Dr. Joycelyn Elders has spent her life involved in the health care of others and brings a unique perspective through her vision of the role of the elderly in the richly textured landscape of America. As a former surgeon general, she has a macro understanding of the needs of the elderly and is a steadfast advocate of health care for all who are a part of this country's fabric. Dr. Robert Coles, drawing on his distinguished experience as a professor of psychiatry at Harvard Medical School and the author of countless books on children, morality, and the social ethics of our culture, explores the contributions of our oldest population and their relevance to the lives of our children through a touching interview he conducted in New Mexico. Chief Arvol Looking Horse, as the spiritual leader of the Lakota Indian tribe, has dedicated his life to preserving his culture whose very foundation was built on the recognition that the spirit of the elderly can light the path for new generations. Lama Surya Das, the most highly trained American lama of the Tibetan tradition of Buddhism, has experienced firsthand the value of learning from those who've spent their lives accumulating wisdom. What he says about how the young among us can learn from the oldest among us is profoundly moving and illuminating. Finally, as a chronicler of the stories of some of the oldest people on earth, I feel privileged to draw back the curtain on their lives and, for the first time, to share the remarkable secrets of their longevity.

PART ONE

Reflections

Being Very Old and Being with the Young

BY ROBERT COLES

EDITOR'S NOTE: *Dr. Robert Coles is a renowned child psychiatrist, Harvard profes-sor, and author of over fifty books, including the Pulitzer Prize-winning, five-volume contemporary classic* Children of Crisis *and the bestselling* The Spiritual Lives of Children. *Reynolds Price has called him "the most eloquent and feeling of American psychiatrists." Dr. Coles has a long and distinguished history of working with the elderly and writing about them. He first encountered the ninety-year-old man discussed in the essay below when he was doing research on the elderly of northern New Mexico in the early 1970s. His book* The Old Ones of New Mexico, *published to acclaim in 1973, contains an essay that first appeared in the* New Yorker *under the title "Una Anciana." The essay's intimate profile of an ordinary woman in her later years was startling to the magazine's readers, who had grown accustomed to its articles about politicians, café society, and celebrities, but had not seen many essays in its pages in the more documentary tradition that was being pioneered by Dr. Coles and Studs Turkel. The response was overwhelmingly positive. Dr. Coles recalls that "like a bolt out of the sky," he received a call from the* New Yorker's *formidable editor-in-chief, William Shawn, who was himself taken aback by the way an article about a simple elderly woman in New Mexico had resonated with his*

sophisticated readership. Later, in a letter to Dr. Coles, Mr. Shawn referred to "the irreg-
ular subject" of this article that had stirred such popular reaction. Just as he did in
"Una Anciana," Dr. Coles evokes in the essay below the extraordinary wisdom that was
to be found in what many may have casually dismissed as just an "ordinary" life.

*   *   *

WHEN I WAS GETTING TO KNOW ELDERLY PEOPLE in New Mexico during the 1970s, I had a lot of medical questions in mind as I talked with those men and women. I also wanted to know how they went about their lives from day to day—doing what, when, where, and with whom or by themselves. I also wanted to hear about their past lives—how things had gone for them, as they traversed through so many years—decades even, of living; and too, I wanted to know what had mattered to them, and still did (their assumptions, values, hopes, worries, the ideals they held high for themselves, for others to hear, notice, take to heart).

In relatively isolated areas of New Mexico, people seemed to cling to the elderly among them as if they were life rafts. For those who were younger, the elders' longevity was evidence that it was possible to survive a great many years despite enormous obstacles. I thought that the respect that the elderly received in these communities was remarkable.

They were ordinary hard-working men and women, who lived in towns north of fancy Santa Fe, in places such as Truchas or El Valle, and these were folks who had struggled long and hard to make a living, keep abreast of bills, attend members of their family, and too, attend the Catholic Church. which they both enjoyed and venerated (though also knew to scrutinize closely, even criticize on occasion). They were men and women whose survival had surprised even themselves, a theme I had heard often, as they looked back, looked around.

Here is a man of ninety speaking about time, its possibilities, its surprises, its burdens, and too, about his daily life (the people and places that are, in their sum signposts of sorts for him, reminders of events ahead in the day—doing what, with whom, and why): "I have been here so long that I think the good Lord has appointed me one of His teachers—the children can see me and talk with me, and when we say good-bye, they have my memories or my lessons learned over all these years in their young, curious minds, always wanting to know about what happened 'back then.' All the time, I hear that: *back then*! So, I tell them about 'back then,' and they listen, and then they have more to ask (and more, and more—until I try to turn things around, get us right here, to this very day that is God's gift to us). When I say that, keep saying that, about God's gift of a day, the children want to know a lot more—about how God makes His decisions, and how we know that they are *His*, and not one of ours! You see how they are wise enough to question me! I think I am still here because the good Lord knows how much these young ones want to know (need to know), and their parents have lots to do, and their teachers at school are as busy as can be, with books to hand out, and the blackboard to fill up, chalk and chalk to wear down, and tests to give (so, who has time to think about God's time, His gift to us of minutes that add and add: they become hours, and the next thing you know a whole day has come and gone).

"Thank the good Lord, by the way, for the nights. 'We sleep to tool up for the day,' my son, an auto mechanic, told his son, and now he tells that to his grandchildren, and I tell them that, too, and for a great-grandfather there are special ears waiting, our priest tells me, because if God has kept me here, it's because he wants children to listen to me, to understand that there is not only today, or yesterday, but so many tomorrows that you have to learn your arithmetic to keep tabs on them. Your life unfolds with each visit of the sun, the moon, my father told me, and I tell the boys and girls that, when I go to Sunday school and let them know what I've watched with my eyes, heard with my ears. They're hungry for answers; I keep saying that I'm looking and listening for those answers—and they can tell that my glasses and my hearing aid are there for a good reason: lots of use, for watching and hearing, so I can learn, be in touch with the world, find the answers for the young.

" 'You're like school, like a library that's a person,' my great-granddaughter told me the other day, and before I fell asleep, I could hear her saying those words to me, a big compliment. I thanked the Almighty for the message one of His creatures passed along! You ask about what is on my mind a lot [as indeed I'd done, yet again, that day] and I know how to give you the right answer: a little girl tells me what I have become for her, and I have been given more than enough: a big meal that tells your body that there's plenty to go do now, with all that energy inside you!"

Silence now, as he moves about, sitting, then adjusts one of his shirt's sleeves—a habit he has: they should be equal in length, each just past the elbow, half way to the wrist. He is attentive to his own clothes, their appearance and how he wears them ("I hold them for others to see," he once said, as he contemplated his small wardrobe) and he is also attentive to the many children who take careful notice of how he dresses: "Young ones want to know where I got this shirt, the pants, the sox. I recall a store that now is gone. I show them a picture of the store; I show them the town when it was smaller, and we all knew each other—who lives here or there; I show them the long ago past; I show them what is no longer, but for me is still there, and is here to share with these children, who are what is ahead, the future. We are here for the ones who come after us—they look to us so they know what life is: 'time builds and builds you,' my granddaughter advised me yesterday. She said I'm like a skyscraper she saw in a book—I've been building and building, I'm that tall! They say children should look up to you, and she was sure saying yes to that, and I was helping her imagine—speak like the Poet the priest says visits us from day to day, helping us to speak—the Lord is the Poet who gives us words (for us to use, to speak)."

The word "speak" prompts him to keep his mouth closed; he looks for the coffee he loves to drink, holds the cup in his hand, enjoys doing so, for a minute or so, remembers when his wife first brought that cup home, and remembers her savoring its warm, exhilarating contents. Yesterday, he told the children about that cup; its history became an aspect of their continuing history lesson, taught by him, called "the elder of elders" by the parish priest, who "keeps joking with me," he continues: "He gives me his views, the priest—that he's no spring chicken, but that with me around, he feels young, ready to laugh and laugh about life. You know what I answer? I tell him he should look at the schoolchildren, on their way to learn in our new school: they make him and me come together—we're both so much older than those boys and girls; we belong to a different time and they belong to what only God knows will be."

He becomes sprightly at the thought of the mention of those children, whom he regards so often and with such knowing respect. Their activities, their comings and goings, keep his senses alive, his head on the alert: their speech, their clothes, their gestures, their playfulness, their spells of boredom, followed by bursts of activity, some of it random, some of it directed at people, places, things, all get him going too. "God provides us with others," he lets his listener know—a brief, pointed summary that he has received from his priest-friend but that he shyly acknowledges to be a part of his own sense of things, long held before this "younger one" came along to minister to a flock of believers. A bit of prodding from the interested recipient of such a comment, and then this: "To say that we live for each other, is to say that we have learned our Bible lessons very well! When I was a boy, my mother, my father, told me that I could learn from them, from teachers at school, but that a wise person looks for a wise person to be his teacher. It didn't take me long to ask the right question. (My parents knew that a good teacher gets a student to ask questions—the better the questions, the better the teacher.) The question was: 'How do you find a wise person, a really wise one?' My mother told me to turn to the Lord above for the answer. My mother would look into space, through the window, her face turned up to the point that I once thought she heard God speak, so that she could give us His advice. She waited long enough for me to want to hear what she was hearing, but of course I never did. Not directly—but you know children are very good at filling in the cracks! I could sense that my mother was bringing me into what she and God together meant! I'm not sure I know how to say it right, but that was what I felt: there is God, and there is my mama, and there is me, and if you start dividing things up, there is wisdom up there, owned by Someone who is older than anyone has ever been (older than this earth we live on, even than the sky, the sun and the stars), and then there is my mama, who seemed plenty old to me, and her mama, who was so old she was called an old one, *the old one*, by everyone, [he had told me that she was nearing the biblical threescore and ten in an earlier conversation], and you know there was someone who was 'older than old,' we called her, and she had seen the first automobile to come hereabouts, not coming down a highway, never mind a paved road, and she owned 'the oldest radio in creation' (we'd hear about it), and I'll tell you, when I was shown it, I thought it can't be true—that sound came out of it, *ever*. (None came out then I'm sorry to say.) But it was held up for us to look at, and to be respectful. 'Be respectful of old things,' mama would tell us; and so you see, we try to look up to *what* was, and of course, *who* was!"

As he fingered old clothes, old appliances, as well as the aforementioned radio, one could readily appreciate how touched he was by such touching—moved, finally, to join himself to such a line-up, such lineage: all those objects, including his body, a memorial to time's occurrence, its passing. Frail, yet steadily determined to get up, move about, he'd take himself to the graves that commemorated the one-time presence of dogs, cats, horses, fowl: "You have to say hello to old friends, to your own kin, to God's kin. 'Remember, child,' my granddaddy said a lot. 'God's kin includes animals as well as people, and, His house includes the land, the trees, the air, the river yonder: if you start messin' with what you've been handed to keep, to enjoy, then you're cutting yourself off, real bad so.' When I remember that advice, these days, I guess I'm talking about myself—I've been here so long that there's no one here who has been here one single day (one single year) longer, so I'm just a part of life that's been here so long it seems like forever to the young ones! That's what my great-grandchildren will tell anyone who listens—that I'm 'so old I must have written those card they buy in the store.' The cards have all those made-up messages that some smart aleck thinks up, to make money for the greeting card companies. I read them, and I want to laugh all the way to the bank, as we used to say (before the banks all failed way back a lifetime ago—it was FDR, we called him, who fixed them, I think, I seem to recall). You know, buying those cards doesn't bring joy—it will do the opposite, put you in debt, so you're in the bank crying, trying for a loan!

"I try to tell young people what we all went through here in America, all over, not only in New Mexico, but throughout 'the 48.' (It's 50 now—I keep up with the numbers, for all my age!) Those young ones, they pay attention when I'm spouting myself off—I think it's their way of figuring things out for themselves. You might say, the older you get, if you're lucky and you still have your wits about you, then the more you've learned from the Lord through being part of His Creation; and a child, he'll know that, she'll know that, in the bones where your body helps you understand.(The other place that's important, it's the heart—'you've got to have heart,' we used to say, my mama and hers before her (going back to way back)."

He seemed himself in another time; his head was lowered. Every once in a while he nodded, then naysayed himself with a shake of the head—until he returned to the two of us there, and in a way, took over for the one paying attention, prodding now and then with a question, a remark, made to prompt further reminiscence, reflection: "I know, you want me to tell you about our children here—we sure have lots of them for you to know! I'm never alone, because they're always about. All the years between me and them—but so much goes back and forth, them talking, chatting away, and me also talking (musing you might say: when you get very, very old, as the kids say I am, then you muse!) I taught then that word 'muse'; my hand was shaking even more, as it does when I try to use that old Parker fountain pen I had—today it's all those instant gadgets they have, no ink required! I taught them by writing down the word 'muse,' one letter at a time: m, u, s, e—that makes muse; to muse means to think about something long enough, deep enough in your thinking head, so you know the word, really do—it's a new-made friend.

"So you know what? One little girl, a friend of my great-granddaughter, here on a visit, said of me: 'He's older than just old.' That girl had been staring at me so hard, I thought I'd be stared down or stared away—looks can kill, you know, but not always; sometimes they just give you your fill, and then they move someplace else with those eyes. When the young really look close at me, I just glance off with my eyes and they get the picture. One girl said to me, 'Big papa, we've kept you far too long!' (They call me that, 'big papa;' I'm only five feet six now, shorter than their parents, a lot of them, and shorter than I used to be, but for them, I'm tall, high tall, in years spent around this town, and that's as 'big' as you can get.) So why not get your eyes filled with someone so old, he's very, very, very, old: that big! You could say that we all want to have someone to look up to—and you get to my age, you're very close to getting to be with the One everyone looks up to, the Maker of all of us. A boy told my grandson once (and he's told it to his son, what he heard) that we all want to hold our heads high, but you shouldn't hold your head too high to yourself—because then you're stuck on yourself; so it's best that you go outside yourself, look up to those older. There's where I'm useful, for people to look up to, and thank me for being here: a link to all that took place so long ago.   I guess there's some religious philosophy there!"

To that his listener said yes, only adding a third word, "psychology": to be quite old is to be an *éminence grise* certainly, but also for many youngsters an entire family's personification, a stretch of time very much present: that time becomes palpably the here-and-now.

The elderly among us have lived long lives of witnessing and experiencing, of truly coming to understand life. They are repositories of knowledge, thoughtfulness, and good judgment. In that sense, they are living gifts to the rest of us. For children, who are trying to explore the world and understand it, the elderly are wonderful teachers. They know life—perhaps better than anyone else would ever come to know it— through their own good luck, endurance, and resiliency. No doubt, that is the explanation for their longevity. And so, they are a gift and a treasure for all of us to hold close and understand. We should all be grateful for them.

Wisdom Keepers: Becoming Elder and Sage

LAMA SURYA DAS, MARCH 2005

To know how to grow old is the master work of wisdom,
and one of the most difficult chapters in the great art of living.

HENRI FREDERIC AMIEL
Swiss critic, 1821–1881

EDITOR'S NOTE: *Lama Surya Das is one of the leading Western lamas and Buddhist teachers. Founder of the Dzogchen Meditation Centers, based in Cambridge, Massachusetts, New York, and Austin, Texas, he leads retreats around the world and is active in interfaith dialogue. Surya Das notes that over the years he has studied with spiritual teachers and gurus in their seventies and eighties in Tibet and India, as well as "elders of the earth who are holders of the mature wisdom of experience and history, and have a larger perspective about age-ing and sage-ing." He is the author of* Awakening the Buddha Within *and other bestselling books. A poet, translator, and chant master, he is also a regular columnist for beliefnet.com, the popular website devoted to religion and spirituality. Surya Das lived in the*

Himalayas for twenty years and in 1993 he joined with the Dalai Lama in founding the ongoing International Western Buddhist Teachers Conferences.

*   *   *

I MET JERRY FRIEDMAN FOR THE FIRST TIME at a picnic at his house in Connecticut on July 4, 2004. I was unprepared to encounter, through his remarkable photos, many of the oldest people on this planet; or their faces, at least, and the stories encoded in them. These are human stories—our stories, yours and mine—the divine comedy of which we are all a part.

For me, that Sunday represented the one day that I had off during a two-week intensive silent Buddhist meditation retreat for my Dzogchen Center that I conduct every summer on the banks of the Hudson River. I had removed my maroon lama robe and was traveling incognito, having donned my Jeffrey Miller Long Island summer costume: shorts, sandals, and a Hawaiian shirt. Jerry, also in shorts, met my wife and me in the backyard of his farmhouse, where a barbecue was in progress. I had heard that Jerry was a strict vegetarian, so we had wondered what kind of fare and fun we'd find at a barbecue chez Jerry on this glorious summer day. Would there be fireworks? Beer?

After we'd met several of Jerry's family and friends, he spirited me into his living room. Before the old stone fireplace, seated on a couch next to a Manhattan real estate executive, I was absolutely riveted as Jerry showed me his slides. Meanwhile, I heard the executive ask when the "celebrated lama author" was coming, even as she unknowingly sat right next to me. I think she was expecting someone dressed up for the clerical role, like the Dalai Lama.

But back to our elders of the earth. As I sat on the couch in the old farmhouse, I was fascinated and delighted when I saw a slide showing the face of the ancient and timeless Mongolian lama Damchaagiin Gendendarjaa, who is certainly the oldest living lama in the world. Jerry tells me this lama is going on 112, according to the elder's seventy-five-year-old daughter, who acted as interpreter for Jerry during his visit to Ulaanbataar. I have known thousands of Buddhist lamas of this world, including the Dalai Lama, whom I have known well and studied with for over three decades. I have known lamas young and old, great and small, male, female—but never have I met such an ancient one of days as Lama Gendendarjaa, who has a Ph.D. of theology diploma hanging on his wall, earned at the age of 106.

I myself am a beneficiary of the wisdom of the elders. During the seventies and eighties in India and the Himalayas, I apprenticed myself to the grand old lamas of Tibet, the last living enlightened masters brought up in fabled Tibet before the

Chinese Communist takeover of 1959. My heart guru Lama Kalu Rinpoche, senior meditation master of the Kagyu School— also the Dalai Lama's yoga teacher—was seventy when I met him in 1973. His face was wrinkled and lined like a road map, yet his energy was brilliant, free and spontaneous, and his sense of humor and play as buoyant and lively as a delighted child's. Even when he traveled around the world and visited my house in Woodstock in July of 1977, he had as much or more energy than I did, although I was ostensibly less than one-third his age in human years. In 1989, I was there at his monastery in the foothills of the Himalayas near Darjeeling, India, when he passed away while sitting up in meditation, and remained so for three days. The light that shone from his eyes the day before he died was the same light that had irradiated him for decades, for centuries—or so they say. Although a skeptic by habit, I found it possible to believe. When I asked the Dalai Lama about these things, he said, "Do you think Lama Kalu was just a man?"

When they die, Tibetan lamas and other accomplished yogis, male and female, intentionally direct their consciousness toward resting in meditative equipoise when the breath ceases, toward the afterlife, and on toward the next life. They are said to choose a favorable rebirth conducive to the continuance of their avowed mission of delivering all beings from the suffering and confusion of worldly existence and on to nirvana. In doing so their mission continues as keepers of an ocean of wisdom— which is what the name Dalai Lama signifies. Thus we have among us today the Fourteenth Dalai Lama, who was recognized at an early age as the reincarnation of his predecessor, after which he was returned to his monastery and his Potala Palace in the Tibetan capital of Lhasa—facts that certainly challenge our ordinary mortal notions of age, aging, and carrying on. Of course this is Buddhist belief, not necessarily yours or many Americans' today, although polls have shown that some 40 percent of Americans do believe in reincarnation. Does this give lie to the old adage that you can't take it with you?

I have known and lived for years with several reincarnated lamas, or *tulkus* as they are called in Tibetan, considered living Bodhisattvas or spiritual saints due to their past life resumes. One of them, I had the privilege to serve as English tutor at his monastery of the Twelfth Gyalwang Drukpa Rinpoche near Darjeeling, when he was ten and eleven years old. Like Mozart, who was prodigiously talented at the age of five, a fact inexplicable unless one considers the possibility of rebirth, the ten-year-old boy prodigy Drukchen Rinpoche that I knew was as spiritually gifted, wise, and seemingly timeless then as the now forty-year-old grand lama who recently visited my retreat center in Austin. So, what does this say about age and longevity, about birth and death, and about the possibilities of spiritual energy and awakened awareness, continuity, lineage, transmission and wisdom-keeping?

Sagacity is the ultimate form of wealth. Wisdom brings peace of mind, compassion, understanding, unselfishness, generosity, and kindness. "Blessed is the man who finds wisdom, who gains understanding; for he is more profitable than silver and yields better returns than gold" (Proverbs 3:13). We would do well to learn from such a spiritual benefactor, regardless of particular religious affiliation, beyond any notion of isms and schisms.

Wisdom can be cultivated, and it can be found within us. Wisdom must be developed if we are to have any significant chance of surviving and flourishing as a race. How to develop it? What is wisdom? Wisdom is knowing reality, just as it is. It includes a higher form of objective judgment coupled with profound discernment, based on an illumined and lucid state of consciousness latent within us all. Tibetan Buddhist teachings tell us that wisdom is developed through three traditional forms of wisdom practices, or phases of true higher education: learning, reflection, and experience, which integrates learning and makes it our own. "Experience, not learning, leads to wisdom and the path to immortality" (William Blake). These practices help us to progress along the continuum from information and knowledge to understanding, insight, experience, and ultimately wisdom—leading directly to inner freedom and spiritual enlightenment. Anyone can become wiser, more unselfish, and loving through such a process. Solomon Ibn Gabriol said, "The first step to wisdom is silence; the second is listening."

Wise words adorn the world for ages.

The sage reads books, hearts and minds, and also opens

The book of nature.

Wisdom is knowing

What matters and what is irrelevant,

What is beneficial and what is not.

It is being fixed on nothing.

Socrates exhorted his pupils to "Know thyself." This is the root of Western philosophy. Philosophy literally means love of wisdom; but what philosophy class today teaches us how to be wiser, more awake, aware, enlightened? I am afraid that today, for the most part, schools teach us how to earn more and not how to keep learning more after graduation, which is a real loss. The best teachers can and should motivate and teach us how to keep learning long after our school days are over, as well as how to find ourselves and our place in life. A true teacher, a wise and authentic elder, is an inspired torchbearer who lights lamps wherever he or she goes, passing the candle flame on; for those who have the good fortune to come into contact with him, a true teacher inculcates leadership and not mere followership. A genuine mentor and spiritual benefactor helps the new generation find their own center—in themselves, not in the master. As Benjamin Disraeli said, "The greatest good you can do for another is not just to share your riches, but to reveal to him his own."

The elders of the earth are a natural resource, and for the most part an untapped one. In these confused, turbulent, and volatile times, at our peril and to the dismay of entire lineages of those who have gone before, we tend to overlook the vast and deep mine of natural wisdom deposits in our very midst. What place does our post-modern society have today for the wise man and the wise woman? Is there an advanced degree of wisdom offered at academic institutions? Is there a department of wisdom or a secretary of enlightenment? The king of the Himalayan Buddhist kingdom of Bhutan mentions measuring the gross national happiness of their country, as we measure the gross national product. What is the goal of life, anyway, if it does not include both individual and collective happiness and inner fulfillment?

Rabbi Nachman of Bratslav said, "The prosperity of a country can be seen simply in how it treats its old people." In Japan, some extraordinarily accomplished people are officially designated national treasures. In America, who recognizes such living treasures? Who considers wisdom preservation or utilizing keepers of wisdom and beacons of enlightenment? Who is the sage laureate? Where is the center for natural resources, the elders? What do I mean by elders as a "natural resource"? I remember a story by Ray Bradbury called "Dandelion Wine." In it, a little boy runs down the street every evening to the porch of his elderly neighbor, a man who is nicknamed The Time Machine, who has stories to tell of olden times. This tale evokes the Nepalese proverb "Sit by a log fire. Listen to an old man."

By contrast, today we all say that our society has little or no appreciation of history, little memory, little knowledge carried over from the past. Perhaps we are a disposable society. We have little or no respect and appreciation for those who have come by the hard-earned accumulation of wisdom, the ultimate form of wealth. We all have heard, as Santayana famously said, that those who don't learn from history are doomed to repeat its mistakes. Once I asked a history professor if there was any evidence that we have learned from history. He said no. Do we have to keep reinventing the wheel in each generation? What is the role for our elders if not to assume the ongoing responsibility for maintaining society's balance and well-being, along with the health and sustainability of our planet and its resources? The Pennsylvania Dutch have a saying: "We grow too soon old and too late smart."

Traditional societies such as those of the old world—like traditional native societies here in the New World, too—have always valued their older people as wisdom-keepers and tribal elders, whose wisdom guided the social order for thousands of years, reaching back past antiquity and far into pre-history. Elders guided the young; the grandmother and grandfather and grand-aunt living side by side with the younger generations helping to bring up the littlest ones on a day-to-day basis, not just on Sundays and the occasional holiday. Traditional elders also provided society with balanced judgment and perspicacity through the accumulated wisdom of experience, playing many different roles, as for example leaders, teachers, bards, shamans and seers, judges, council members. By respecting and venerating the elders, as well as their wise men and wise women who have kept alive the flame of tradition, culture, history, legend, and always the most profound wisdom of the ancients, these societies, tribes, clans, and even civilizations have collectively ensured their continuance into the future. By appreciating cultural wisdom and wealth, including the past, they deliver traditional knowledge relevantly into the present. This is the necessity of the oft-lost and overlooked treasure called lineage.

Yet, how to become a wise elder and not just an old fool? How to extract the nutrients, the wisdom deposits, from the lessons of life and not just become a jaded old curmudgeon who has seen it all and knows it all, is bored, worn out, and wonders, "Is this all?" And questions, "What, if anything, is next?"

In traditional cultures with a strong spiritual foundation, age is associated with maturity and insight rather than with either senility or success, and the second half of life is a time for deepening reflection and inner self-discovery. Aging rounds off the rough corners and allows us to become deeper and more harmonious. "The impermanence of the body should give us great clarity, deepening the wonder in our senses and eyes of this mysterious existence we share and are surely just traveling through" (Hafiz, fourteenth century, Persia). Even spiritual realization ripens over time. In Buddhism, meditation and a certain perspective on awareness, consciousness, energy, and spirit include not just a particular formal contemplative activity, but also an outlook on life that matures with age like a good wine.

"The strategy of successful aging is an admirable and fulfilling one as long as it lasts; the only drawback is that it's destined to fail," writes Stephan Bodian in a *Yoga Journal* article on conscious aging. "Eventually, our accustomed activities lose their capacity to satisfy us or require too much energy to sustain. What happens when we can no longer mountain bike, walk long distances, play golf, drive a car? What deeper source of happiness and satisfaction can we draw on then? The great Tibetan Buddhist master Kalu Rinpoche once said that the reason we suffer as we age is that we're attached to the same pleasures and activities we enjoyed in our youth. In the end, despite our best efforts, nearly every one of us will decline, weaken, grow sick, and die." It is in our own higher self-interest to learn how to appreciate the virtues of adversity, how to gain from loss and change, and how to let go of the person we used to be, in order to find out who we really are and can be.

My old friend Ram Dass writes, in *Aging Body, Timeless Soul*: "It turns out that the solution to the problem of change is yet another change. But what we're changing this time is who we see ourselves to be. That is, we don't have to go on clinging to the past, buying into a cultural myth of The Youthful Me, and hanging on to who we used to be. We don't have to go on identifying ourselves with that being who's changing, seeing the aging process through those eyes. Just behind all that drama is a place of mind-fulness, a place of the witness. It is a part of us that is purely equanimous, that's just watching the whole story unfold. That's what I'll call the soul....Looking at our lives from the soul-perspective doesn't just give us a more effective way of fulfilling our roles—it takes us outside of our roles. The soul-view gives us a look at our lives from the outside, and that puts a different light on things."

In *The Insecurity of Freedom*, the distinguished rabbi, author, and human rights activist Abraham Joshua Heschel writes: "One ought to enter old age the way one enters the senior year at a university. The years of old age may enable us to attain the high values we failed to sense, the insights we have missed, and the wisdom we ignored. They are indeed formative years, rich in possibilities to unlearn the follies of a lifetime, to see through inbred self-deceptions, to deepen understanding and compassion, to widen the horizon of honesty, to redefine the sense of fairness." These are words of a true elder and sage. Robert Greenleaf points out in *The Power of Servant Leadership* that preparing for old age and using these formative years allows elders to serve in a way not possible for the young or middle-aged among us. Elders have a unique place and role in the Great Mixture, a place for service beyond house-holding and maintaining a career.

Spirit can be said to be the driving force behind the motive to serve. And the ultimate test for spirit in one's old age is, I believe, this: can one look back at one's active life and achieve serenity from the knowledge that one has served? And can one regard one's present state, no matter how limited by age and health, as one of continuing to serve? One of Greenleaf's deeply etched memories is the view of an old man of ninety-five sitting by the window of his fisherman's house on the far-out coast of Maine quietly knitting nets for lobster traps that the active fisherman in the family would use. He was still serving with what he could do best at his age. At age seventy-five, when Greenleaf finally stopped traveling, he had come to realize that he could no longer serve by carrying on such an active role in the world. "I would only get in the way if I tried. Now, I came to accept, I can best serve by being. "Lounge and invite the soul," as Whitman said.

In Hong Kong in the mid-seventies, my Chinese friend Michael Lee—an aged puppet-maker and longtime Zen-man, originally from Shanghai—told me his favorite Taoist story: One day some disciples found the Taoist philosopher Chuang Tzu in front of his house, sitting peacefully on the ground in the sun with his freshly washed long hair cascading down around him. The students gathered around him and waited patiently for Chuang Tzu—who often quoted Lao Tzu (whose name means old master) and commented on his pithy aphorisms while teaching. "What are you doing, Master?" they finally asked. "Drying my hair in the sun," the old sage replied. "Can we help you?" they wanted to know. "How can you help me; what is there that I need to do? The hair is being dried by the sun, and I am resting at the origin of all things." For me this story enigmatically points out how to journey to the very center of things, beyond the dichotomy of doing and being and yet including both. The Taoist sages exemplify harmony, serenity, flow.

I was in Hawaii on the island of Maui for a retreat last winter, and heard the aged slack key guitar master George Kahumoku, Jr., play, sing, and tell stories from his book *A Hawaiian Life*. He told one tale about his old aunt on the Big Island, who had taught him the unique slack key style when he was a young boy. "She always played the same song over and over. Later, when I was a teenager and had lots of tunes in my repertoire, I was bold enough to ask her, 'Auntie, why don't you play something different? You know many tunes; why keep playing the same thing?' She answered: 'You are young, you like new things and many different ones. That's fine. I am old now; our old Hawaiian tradition is to like one thing a lot, and go all the way into it.'"

Let's think together for a moment about the wisdom of experience. We all have lots of experiences, whatever age we may be; every day, every hour is a treasure trove. We grow old—if we're lucky, that is, and don't poop out prematurely—and somehow, some become wise elders and others just become older. What makes us think it is too late to be of value, just because we have traversed many fairways and reached the back nine of life? Perhaps we just get younger and more youthful in spirit every year after the big five-o is reached, until we become like children again, and then like babies, and then finally are just like a gleam in our father's eye. As one of my erstwhile gurus, Mae West, said, "You're never too old to grow younger."

Twelve hundred years ago in Tibet, Mipham Gonpo was eighty years old before he met a spiritual teacher. As soon as his karmic seeds and latent spirituality were awakened by hearing Buddhist wisdom from his guru, Vairotsana the Translato (one of Tibet's first enlightened masters), he started to meditate. The old man was so infirm he couldn't keep his body upright; so his master provided him with a chinstick to prop him up in the seated position, a little crutch placed like a table leg beneath his chin. Mipham Gonpo meditated for some years, became enlightened, and lived to the ripe old age of 120, benefiting and awakening many disciples. The moral of the story is: Who can say it is too late or too early? What is time anyway, but a mental construct, a fabrication—a mere matter of relativity.

When I worked for a few years in the old-age homes and nursing homes of Ulster County in the late seventies, many residents described to me their painful feelings of having outlived their usefulness and productive, meaningful time on earth, and of being cast aside as burdens in our youth-oriented society and fast-paced, technologically oriented over-information age and hyper-modern world. I was a teacher then, but they taught me! It was a real eye-opening, heart-opening experience, which I have never forgotten.

Ram Dass told a story about Frances, a resident in a nursing home, who said, "Lack of physical strength keeps me inactive and often silent. They call me senile, but senility is just a convenient peg on which to hang nonconformity. A new set of faculties seems to be coming into operation. More than at any other time of my life, I seem to be aware of the beauties of our spinning planet and the sky above. Old age is sharpening my awareness." In other words, what appears to be loss may in fact be transformation, if we allow the mind to change without fear.

Our sequestered and institutionalized elder population is rich with the experiences of parents and teachers, artists and executives, engineers and attorneys, doctors and nurses; citizens who could easily be employed and occupied for mutual benefit. What major charity or volunteer organization is consciously, intentionally trying to mine those deep reserves? Today with the Internet and other modern forms of electronic communication, elders have even more chance to stay connected, to participate and communicate, and to keep learning and even earning, even those who may be homebound or living in elder facilities—opportunities and challenges not readily available to the senior citizens I worked with in Ulster County. At the age of ninety-three, Pablo Casals was practicing the cello five or six hours a day. Someone asked him, "Pablo, why are you still practicing the cello? You're ninety-three!" Casals answered, "Because I think I'm making some progress."

The elderly are the fastest-growing segment of our population. Gerontologist Ken Dychwald says we are about to experience an Age Wave. Today the average life expectancy is seventy-five, and the National Institute of Aging predicts that soon life expectancy will be eighty-six years for men and nearly ninety-two years for women. One hundred years ago, 2.4 million Americans or less than 4 percent of the population were over sixty-five; today there are more than 35 million over that age and the number keeps growing as the baby boomers come of elder age, bulging the bell curve. With our current stereotypes about old age, our low expectations of this population, our misperception that anyone over sixty-five should be put out to pasture, who among us is guiding them toward successful conscious aging and growth at the sage-ing age? Who is helping them continue their physical vigor, intellectual activity, and meaningful service of some kind? Isn't it our loss to relegate the elderly to a nonpro-ductive, nonparticipatory place in our great democracy?

In the sixth century BC, the great Taoist philosopher Lao Tzu was the keeper of the Royal Archives at Loyang. He was retiring from this world and leaving China forever, riding out through the Western Pass into the wilderness, when the gatekeeper stopped him and requested the old sage's final words of wisdom. It was only then that The old master extemporaneously penned his timeless classic, *Tao Te Ching (The Way and Its Power/Virtue)*, which has often been called the wisest book in the world and, along with the Bible and the Bhagavad Gita, is the most translated. Imagine if the old master hadn't written anything down for posterity, or if those six thousand calligraphed characters—comprising eighty-one verses or poems in all—had not been preserved over the past 2,500 years. The great Confucius, who as a young man met the old master once, said that Lao Tzu was like a magnificent dragon whom no one could encompass.

The historical Buddha (563–483 BC) taught all over northern India from the age of thirty-five until the age of eighty. The seminal Chinese Zen master Joshu started teaching when he was eighty, and lived to be one hundred. Grandma Moses was eighty when she sold her first painting and 25 percent of her paintings were done after she was a hundred years of age. Benjamin Franklin was seventy-eight when he invented bifocals and eighty-one when he helped frame the U.S. Constitution. Goethe was eighty-one when he finished writing *Faust*. Albert Schweitzer was still performing operations in his African hospital at age eighty-nine.

As people transition into life's latter decades, cycling into what sociologists iden-tify as the third age, they need what Zalman Schachter-Shalomi in *From Age-ing to Sage-ing* calls "a psycho spiritual model of development that enables them to com-plete their life journey, harvest the wisdom of their years, and transmit a legacy to future generations. Without envisioning old age as the culminating stage of spiritual development, we short-circuit this process and put brakes on the evolutionary imperative for growth that can be unleashed by our increased longevity." Who today has time and space to stop and look deeper into any one thing, harvesting the wisdom of longevity, with so much activity, outer and inner, constantly competing for our attention? Let me put forth the notion—and I am certainly not the first to say this— that true elders represent those who take the time to focus on exploring life more deeply than most, and who remain among us to tell the tale. If only we would listen.

Tibet is the last old wisdom–based culture to have survived since ancient times. Buddhism is older than both Christianity and Islam. As a Buddhist monk living in monasteries in the Himalayas, I spent most of my time at the feet of sage old gurus, both male and female. I love to visit not only man's ancient sacred shrines and museums around the globe, but also the thousand-year-old grove of redwood trees in the Pacific Northwest—a living cathedral—and the long-lived sea turtles of the Galapagos. But above all, I revere the wisdom of the ancients, who have mulched the treasure trove of wisdom over time and have preserved and transmitted it for our unending benefit. It is my great hope to live long enough to pass on to the next generations an offering of whatever wisdom I have been fortunate enough to gather and make my own—paying back my own gracious spiritual teachers and benefactors.

The Earth's Elders project represents something far better than collective amnesia and shortsightedness, providing a viable link to both our past and future, in the multilayered richness and diversity of our very present. I think meeting the earth's elders presents a unique opportunity for young people of all ages to learn something edifying and also to contribute. The story that these aged and timeless faces tell is our story—your story, my story. You, too, are part of it. In turn, as you make your way through life and find your own voice, you will tell your story, yet to be written.

We are the elders and sages now; we are the ancestors for generations yet to come. We must awaken the sage and leader within, harvesting what wisdom we can and passing it on to the next generations. We can do that in innumerable ways, great and small, through modeling a wise, healthy, balanced, and beautiful way of life. Through teaching, parenting, mentoring, inspiring, motivating, volunteering, healing, helping—that is, being of service wherever and whenever we can—we can be genuine benefactors to the young'uns, lighting their lamps so they may carry them forth into the world, their world.

The sage loves, trusts, and accepts others; therefore, others trust and accept him. A sage befriends herself, and is thus the friend of one and all. The wise know reality and comprehend their place in the world, the universe, and in the cosmos—understanding life's big questions. The wisdom of the elders brings love, harmony, and contentment, the greatest form of wealth to our midst.

We are all going to die, but who among us is going to truly live? Let us strive to leave this benighted world a more beautiful place than we found it, and become like beacons illumining the darkness of confusion and illusion, exemplifying a sane, wise, compassionate way of life.

Let go of selfishness and you will be as if immortal.

It's not what happens to us but what we make of it

That makes all the difference;

We can't control the wind, but we can

Learn to set our sails and navigate better.

Like in baseball, in golf;

our grip determines our swing and our play.

What we seek

Is not outside ourselves, so we can obtain it.

It is so close, we overlook it.

Understanding the world

is knowledge;

Knowing yourself is true wisdom.

Wisdom tells me I am

as nothing; love tells me everything.

LAMA SURYA DAS

Health and Health Care

JOYCELYN ELDERS

EDITOR'S NOTE: *Dr. M. Joycelyn Elders was the first African-American in history and only the second woman to serve as the surgeon general of the Public Health Service of the United States. Her life story is an inspiring triumph over numerous obstacles. As the great-granddaughter of slaves, she grew up in poverty in rural Arkansas. She never saw a doctor until she went to college and yet she became one of the most esteemed pediatric endocrinologists in the country. When she went to the University of Arkansas Medical School (UAMS) in 1956, she was the only black woman in her class. After obtaining her medical degree, Dr. Elders completed her internship at the University of Minnesota Hospital and her residency at the University of Arkansas Medical College, and earned an M.S. in biochemistry in 1967. She joined the faculty at UAMS as a professor of pediatrics and was board certified in pediatric endocrinology in 1978. Dr. Elders was appointed by then-Governor Bill Clinton to the post of Director of the Arkansas Department of Health in 1987. She served with distinction, and her accomplishments included providing health care to poor communities, expanding the state's prenatal care program, and increasing the number of children who received immunizations. After serving as surgeon general in 1994, Dr. Elders returned to the University of Arkansas, where she continued to teach. She has received numerous awards for her humanitarian work and coura-geous advocacy of public health. In 1996, her acclaimed memoir,* Joycelyn Elders, M.D., *was published. Now retired from practice, she is professor emeritus at the University of Arkansas School of Medicine and continues to be a popular public speaker and vocal advocate for children's rights.*

*   *   *

WE VIEW THE SAGES AMONG US, our precious earth elders who abound with understanding of life, more as oddities of nature than sources of wisdom. They uniquely posses a sagacity for which the younger of us can only strive. It is astonishing and perplexing that this invaluable resource, brought about by incredibly varied and numerous experiences of long life, remains virtually untouched, untapped, untried, and sometimes not tolerated by our culture.

While we drill and utilize all oil, gold, and diamond resources as possible, we squander the incalculably valuable wisdom of our earth elders. They have much more to offer us in terms of productivity, information, and understanding regarding improving the quality of life for all than we have yet imagined.

They often move among us unnoticed, waiting to be asked to participate at the table of our culture.

If people in Leonardo da Vinci's time valued his inventions and discoveries instead of ignoring and ridiculing them, how much more advanced would our civilization be in terms of science and engineering? If we were to utilize the resources of our earth elders instead of dismissing them, how much more advanced would our civilization be in virtually every area of life?

The past and projected growth of the population age sixty-five and over affects virtually every corner of our society, including challenges first of all to the aging individuals themselves, government at all levels, families, and health care systems to meet the needs of the older population.

The number of older Americans increased from 3.1 million in 1900 to 35.6 million in 2003.[1] By the year 2030, the older population will more than double to 71.5 million when it is projected that 20 percent of Americans will be sixty-five and over. Presently in the United States, the number of people aged sixty-five years or older is about one in eight. This is an increase of 3.3 million people or 10.2 percent since 1992. The U.S. Census Bureau projects that the population age eighty-five and over could grow from 4.2 million in 2000 to nearly 21 million by 2050.[2]

These increased years given to us are a wonder of human achievement and a great gift of life that bring challenges we have never before faced.

Some of these challenges include:

⋗ The economic, social, and cultural implications of the older population becoming a larger percentage of the population as a whole.

⋗ Good health practices becoming an essential element of American lifestyle throughout the life cycle. This includes educating the entire populace at an early age to make healthy choices. Most of our earth elders have followed the seven characteristics of healthy people, which are 1) to eat breakfast, which many of us skip; 2) to consume a high-fiber, low-saturated-fat diet distributed among three meals and two snacks per day; 3) to exercise at least twenty minutes five days per week; 4) to consume no more than two alcoholic beverages per day for men or one for women; 5) to get six to eight hours of sleep daily; 6) to practice safe sex; 7) to maintain an ideal body weight.

⋗ Providing affordable, accessible, appropriate, and preventive health care throughout life beginning with prenatal care and continuing through life to older age.

⋗ Promoting social interaction and integration in order to improve intergenerational harmony and create a more socially responsible culture.

⋗ The elimination of physical and emotional elder abuse, age discrimination, and discrimination against persons who are impoverished financially.

⋗ Providing social services for poor, disadvantaged, and disabled older persons.

⋗ Making the decision that government has responsibility for the welfare of all its population.

⋗ Our greatest and most important challenge may be the acceptance of the imperative to alter our value system for the inclusion of earth elders and others who are older and may be impoverished, who add worth to our society without contributing financially. All the preceding changes will come about naturally if we can achieve this final one.

Every gift brings a new responsibility. The gift of extended life expectancy for a whole population brings a new dynamic to all our lives. We need discussions concerning the enormous opportunities this brings us as well as the need to change our ways to accommodate and utilize this valuable gift for the advantage of all.

Opportunities for living life fully exist in old age as much as in youth. As Longfellow put it in verse, "And as the evening twilight fades away / The sky is filled with stars, invisible by day" ("Morituri Salutamus," 1874). Earth elders have priceless experience and wisdom to add to the cultural richness of all of us. We can listen to them and learn.

The older population is a diverse group who experience a varying need for dependency upon external support. Some are able, fit, and in good health while others are not. In 2003, 38.6 percent of noninstitutionalized older persons (65+) assessed their health as excellent or very good (compared to 66.6 percent for persons aged 18–64).[3] Some have support groups such as family with whom they live or who live nearby. Some enjoy the benefit of belonging to a cultural group that values its older folk.

While the percentage of the older population with disability increases with age, the percentage that does not require assistance for these disabilities is about 65 percent for persons over age 80 years and about 92 percent for those who are in the 65–69 age group. Therefore, most seniors are able to live at least fairly independent lives. Of course, it is preferable to live among friends and family for most folk.

The elderly population who live in rural areas are among the poorest and often most vulnerable, being isolated from family and friends as well as facing diminished accessibility to health care. We live in the richest country in the world, which boasts possession of 25 percent of the wealth of the world, yet it is owned by only 5 percent of the U.S. population. Inexplicably, more than 44 million people, or 18.6 percent of our population of 294 million people, do not have access to health care. Access includes provider access, financial access, cultural access, and transportation access.

Our health care system needs to be coherent, comprehensive, cost effective, equitable, universal, and offer a choice of providers. However, we know that it does not have all of these characteristics. Individuals who are most disenfranchised are our very young, very old, and/or poor, often living in rural or inner-city areas. We need a health care system that provides high-quality, cost-effective, timely, patient-centered care, which is safe, effective, and equitable. In fact, our health care system is not a health care system at all. Rather, it is a very expensive sick care system. We spend 15 percent of our Gross Domestic Product (GDP) on health care, yet our health care system ranks fifty-seventh in overall goodness and fairness, being most unfair to our most vulnerable citizens.

According to the *British Medical Journal*, "Accumulating research evidence indicates that the greater the income gap between the poorest and the wealthiest in a society, the higher the death rates for infants and adults and the lower the life expectancy for all members of that society, regardless of [Socio-Economic Status] SES.3."

Educational attainment influences socioeconomic status, which in turn plays a role in well-being at older ages. Higher levels of education are usually associated with higher incomes, higher standards of living, and above-average health.

In our culture, capitalists (who are few) are valued for life even into old age, whereas workers (who are many) are valued only as long as they actively participate in the economic system as workers. In short, the very nature of our economic system may provoke disrespectful responses toward those who do not contribute as active participants in the system, because it is my opinion that how we identify ourselves has more to do with our capitalistic economic system than any other trait.

The *British Medical Journal* also notes, "Income distribution may be a proxy for other social indicators, such as degree of investment in human capital. Communities that tolerate large degrees of inequality in income may . . . [also] tend to under invest in social goods such as public education or accessible health care." [4]

Do older persons have rights? If they do, what are those rights?

Some groups of Americans are at greater risk of material hardship concerning the necessities of life than others are, due to changes in the economy or other social conditions. These groups, which include the elderly, find that public opinion, social conditions, lack of inclusion in decisions, lack of accessible information about how the systems are designed to help them, and discrimination all work effectively to exclude many from taking advantage of assistance that is in place and due to them.

Preparing for good health in old age is an issue that we usually only begin to think about when we approach a time when our bodies begin to stop operating as well as they did. For instance, our first thoughts of aging may be something like "I don't remember grunting like this when I get out of my car" or maybe "I used to like baths but my bathtub is just too difficult to get out of, so I have to take a shower." We wonder why we are so stiff in the mornings. The street signs seem to have been replaced by smaller ones. Why would the city do that? Chairs seem lower—especially the toilet.

Some people become obsessed with their wrinkles. However, it seems to me that it was God's infinite wisdom to arrange it so that our eyesight dims just about the time our faces wrinkle. Therefore, when we gaze into the mirror in the morning, we think we look pretty much the same for quite some years. Accepting the vagaries of health may assist us in living long lives. While it is never too late to seek health in our lives, sooner is better than later. Better late than never, but better early than late.

It does not appear clear to me that, as a society, we have decided that government bears responsibility for the welfare of all its people. There are too many Americans in poverty without medical care, housing, food, education, and all the essentials of life. These people are injured, disabled, young, old, and physically and/or emotionally sick. It just seems obvious that, as a nation, we have not made the commitment to Americans who are lacking some of the essentials for life. Before we can begin to prepare plans—much less implement them—Americans themselves must make a decision that the government is responsible at least to some degree.

If we are not able to say that our government represents us, or at the very least should be reflective of our wishes and bears responsibility for the welfare of Americans, then we are a lost cause. What good is government if it is not supportive of all the people it governs? To whom is it responsible? If it is responsible only to those participating positively at any given moment in its economy, then we are barbarous. Grocers, other retailers, the IRS, and those who take the money of the poor do not refuse that kind of participation by anyone. It is only when government does not provide medical care and the essentials of life in some way for those who are the most vulnerable, that problems arising from our indecision to help come into play. There are Americans who cannot bring themselves to offer a helping hand to others. They have not made the decision that they, as individuals or collectively through their government, are responsible to all—even its poorest and most vulnerable. When we do make that decision to include all at our bounteous table (for I am hopeful that we will), then we can finally call this a civilized place and a just society.

We will need to develop new policies across many cultural, age, and health borders. It will be as if we were in the sixties—planning to go to the moon without knowing how. It will be an achievement no less noble and astonishing than putting a human being on Mars.

In developing these new policies, strategies, and programs, the needs and preferences of older people, especially those who are poor, must to be taken into account. Therefore, it is essential that we ask and listen to those whose futures we are planning. All the consequences of the implementation of these policies and programs must be evaluated.

While aging is irreversible (what sage would wish it to be?), attitudes are not. New positive images of aging can carry our society into a glorious new dimension. Our earth elders can guide us toward not only a description of what we want to accomplish in seeking a more just and civilized place to live, but they can lead us on the road that will help us to get from here to there. If we are wise, we will listen, and then take action.

Great-Aunt Anna's Old-Age Secrets

DR. ELDERS'S GREAT-AUNT ANNA

1. Great-Aunt Anna always said it is important to remember that even unhealthy people can live a long time. She recalled always being a little sickly, even as a baby. She just managed to take care of herself and live a very long time (almost to 106). She lived alone in her own home, taking care of her housework, preparing meals, doing grocery shopping and most of the yard

work, including gardening, until she was almost 102. When she fell and was injured, her son thought she needed to be in a nursing home.

2. She said she always believed in eating slowly. When she was a teacher, sometimes she took just a hard-boiled egg to school for lunch. However, it always took her one whole hour to eat it. Whatever she ate, she ate it very slowly.

3. Aunt Anna believed in oatmeal; she had a bowl every single day. She said that she didn't know what nutritional power it had, but one day someone would discover what it was. And they have! Oats have been found to lower cholesterol and to prevent some cancers.

4. She also believed in having one large glassful of her own "put up" tomato juice daily. She knew that there was some nutritional power in that as well. She was correct. Canned tomato products have been found to be very beneficial in cancer prevention and in building a healthy immune system. She almost never drank coffee and preferred tea, which has antioxidants and cleans teeth in a way that protects against cavities.

5. Aunt Anna believed in prayer and meditation and devoted several hours every afternoon to this purpose. Meditation for twenty minutes a day has been shown to lengthen life.

6. She played the piano and sang every day. Singing boosts endorphin production, and exercises the soft palette (which diminishes snoring) and vocal chords to keep a young-sounding voice. It also increases lung capacity, producing more oxygen for more brainpower.

7. Aunt Anna devised her own exercise program. In the mornings after she awoke, she exercised for thirty minutes in bed. Then, after rising, she exercised forty-five more minutes. She flailed her arms about, bent around, marched around the room, and did all sorts of exercises I have never seen. She said she had devised them over many years to stretch what needed stretching and to strengthen all her muscles. At night before bed, she reversed the exercise program, beginning first in her living room, and then doing more in bed.

8. She took only one pill a day for her glaucoma, never anything else.

9. She laughed a lot and walked to church for every service; it was just behind her home. Her doctor told her when she was in her twenties that she had such bad eyes that she would likely become blind in her later years. So, she memorized chapters from the Bible and memorized poems and other writings that

were important to her. When her eyes did fail, she still was able to present programs at church and give speeches because of the material she had committed to memory.

10. Aunt Anna liked to visit the patients at the "old folks home," as she called it. She enjoyed recounting one day when she was visiting there with the pastor. A little old lady grasped her hand as she walked past. She exclaimed to Aunt Anna in a quaky little voice, "Honey, today is my birthday, and I am seventy-five years old. Can you believe that?" Aunt Anna, who was in her nineties, just smiled sweetly and offered congratulations,

11. Aunt Anna believed in purpose in life. She felt that to have a meaningful life required that one should have purpose and act on that purpose. Her purpose was spirituality and music. When she was a little girl, she wanted to be a foreign missionary to China. However, her father told her that he just didn't know how to help her work out that goal. So, she married a Methodist clergyman and convinced him to minister to the poor people in rural Arkansas. At each church to which they were appointed, she taught children, mostly girls, how to play the piano, sing, read, and speak in public. It was a difficult life of service during the Great Depression. She had only one child and almost died giving birth. The churches couldn't pay Uncle Claude's compensation in money so they brought the family a little food they could spare sometimes and shared their old clothing. Great-Aunt Anna used to say, "Find what your purpose is in life and follow it with all you heart."

12. Aunt Anna always began the day as though she were having guests. She fixed her hair and put on a fresh dress, usually with a pretty pin. She always wore hose.

13. Aunt Anna had many friends who visited her frequently and she visited them. They had tea. She gave away most of the paltry income she had; she always seemed to find people who needed it more than she did. She graduated from the high school, which was across the street from the house where she and Uncle Claude ultimately moved after retiring from the ministry. There were three people in her graduating class, three women. When two of them met in the post office, which was frequently, they joked that most of their class was there, so they might as well have a reunion. All three were long lived. They each had only one child.

14. Aunt Anna's son and his family lived in another state, but visited frequently. There were some members of her family in that little town for a few

years. However, many of her years, and all of her last years, were spent without any family members in town. Her church was supportive and so were her friends.

15. She felt secure in knowing that if she needed to go to a doctor, she could. She went only rarely because she said that there was little they could do for any of her problems. When she was in her nineties, she couldn't decide whether or not to have cataract surgery because she didn't know how much longer she would live anyway. I suggested that since she didn't know, she might as well have as much eyesight as possible. After the surgery, she was ordered to rest for several weeks without exercising. She quickly realized that if she didn't exercise, she would lose her mobility. So, she gradually returned to her daily schedule of exercising.

16. She had a positive outlook on life and was very good at substituting something she could have for something she wanted but couldn't have. She did not have the opportunity to travel around the world, but she said she could watch TV programs about nature and travel, which she enjoyed tremendously.

17. She was not an uproarious person who joked all the time; rather, she had a happiness that could be described as serenity. However, she and her long-lived brother, Uncle Edbert, laughed hilariously at practical jokes and enjoyed the silliness they had together.

18. Aunt Anna had chickens and liked gardening and growing things. This kept her in touch with nature and gave her something to share with her friends and neighbors.

19. She said that neither her mother nor her father ever lifted a hand against her. Neither did either of them ever raise their voice to her in anger. I think this may have given her a gentle nature that set her off well on a happy road throughout her life.

Sacred Thoughts

ARVOL LOOKING HORSE

EDITOR'S NOTE: *In 1966, when Chief Arvol Looking Horse was only twelve years old, he was chosen to be the nineteenth-generation keeper of the Sacred White Buffalo Calf Pipe of the Lakota, Dakota, and Nakota Great Sioux Nation, a sacred honor that had never before been bestowed on one so young. Raised by his grandparents, Chief Arvol immersed himself in the traditions, history, and language of his people on the Cheyenne River Reservation in South Dakota. Now, as a spiritual leader of the Sioux Nation, Chief Arvol dedicates himself to the goal of world peace, unity, and the healing of his people. He is a member of the Board of the Society of Peace and Prayer, which travels around the world planting peace poles that bear the inscription "May Peace Prevail on Earth." Chief Arvol has spoken at the White House and at the United Nations, and has traveled to South Africa to meet with Desmond Tutu. In 1995, he met with the Dalai Lama to express the Lakota Nation's support for Tibet. An internationally respected leader in the area of human rights, Chief Arvol is the guiding force behind World Peace and Prayer Day, celebrated annually on June 21. In 1996, he received the prestigious Canadian Wolf Award, which honors those (like the award's first recipient, Nelson Mandela) who have devoted themselves to the cause of peace. He has also received numerous other awards for his efforts to promote global healing. Chief Arvol's impassioned writings have drawn attention to the urgent need to recognize and respect diversity, preserve sacred sites and indigenous religious freedom, and to create a legacy that will restore peace to all peoples on the planet. He has also sought to protect the ancient sacred ceremonies of his ancestors and to have the United States government honor the original treaties that were signed by his forefathers*

*   *   *

ALL OF OUR TRADITIONS are oral traditions and teachings that were handed down from our grandparents. I was raised by my grandfather and my grandmother. I was taught mostly in the evenings. My grandfather would wake me up and help me meet the day. His way was a gentle way. He would say, "*Ta-ko-s'a* (grandchild), let's go now." We would go to bed when the sun went down. During the day we would haul water and chop wood; it was up to us to work. There were days when my grandparents would explain how to use medicines, what berries to use. They taught me the different seasons for picking the berries to make certain medicines. They also taught me how to pick. One day my grandmother told me to go and pick some chokecherries by the river. First, she said, go up to the berries against the wind and ask for them in a good way. Then go with the wind on your back and don't ask and just take. Then she had me taste them, and the ones that I picked against the wind were sweet and the ones that were picked with the wind against my back were bitter.

Back then, it was expected that your grandparents educated you. But it is no longer that way. Times have changed. The modern society changed our traditions and culture. Our old people are now being put into old-age manors. We no longer have respect and honor for grandparents and the life wisdom they have earned.

When I was twelve years old, I remember my grandmother passing into the spirit world. At that time, the Bundle that I carry was chosen from a dream that my grandmother had. The Bundle is a spirit that chooses the keeper, so before a person dies, they have a dream who the next keeper is. It skipped my father, my older brother, and chose me. So they had a big ceremony. Because I was twelve years old, the People had a coming of age ceremony and it was then I received the sacred Bundle, which has in it the sacred pipe. I thought this was something for our family, but later I realized that this Bundle was to keep for the whole nation. In that time of the coming of age, each elder talked to me one by one and the *i-ni-pi* (purification) ceremony was done, which was a long ceremony, and then they had a feast. There are a lot of things I would like to explain, but we have reached a fine line, so we can only speak so much. The teaching does not let me go into all that happens, but it was an all-day ceremony. It is important to really understand the responsibility of the man. The women have their own ceremony and their own teachings. What I can tell you is that the elders talked to me about the energy of life. From the moment a child is born, to everything that has an energy, a spirit, even a blade of grass has a spirit and energy from Mother Earth. My grandmother told me about this energy, you have to respect it. She told me that you can't use foul language or carry a weapon, because those things carry energy that can hurt people. I am the nineteenth keeper and nothing has changed. We have changed the way we dress, the things that we eat, and the way that we live, but there are some things in the ceremonies we should never change. This is important. We cannot skip over things or the ceremonies will lose their power to heal our People. We are hoping to bring the ceremonies back, because we seem to have lost so much of what it really meant to be who we are as a People.

Long ago, when a child was born and raised, the most important teachings of our elders were learned from a baby. The elders were part of their lives and it was full. We had so much respect for our ancestors and our grandmothers and grandfathers. But today there is so much abuse of them, because hardly anyone goes through the ceremonies that teach the cycle of life and how it should be respected. This was broken and our traditions have changed, because we are caught up in this very fast world. Today the mother and the father have to work. There is no time for the children. In our tradition, when a child is born, then the mother has to nurse the baby. This is done out of love and compassion. Sometimes the baby was nursed for three or four years; that seems too old, but back then the mothers understood, because the baby needed the attention or the nutrition to help it become strong. Back then nobody made fun of that, but today the babies are being bottle-fed, so the bond becomes weaker and there's no love or care. We think we're giving love with money, but something is not there. The tradition is to nourish the child. In order to renourish the children, we need to bring back the old traditions.

Patience was taught at an early age. At our family's home, west of my community, there is a place called *wam-bli o-ku-ya*, a butte where they catch the eagle. A pit is dug and covered with branches. Then a rabbit or some kind of bait is laid on top. A young boy has to sit there, quiet, sometimes for a day until the eagle comes. You have to be swift to catch it. That's where they see if the boy has patience, courage, and swiftness. He has to catch the eagle, pull a tail feather, and let the eagle free. A lot of our children are into candy and sugar and it makes them hyper. They don't know how to sit still. A lot of the things we love to eat are affecting us today. We see the traditional basic food as a medicine. We tell our people we must eat the foods in our traditional way that makes us healthy. Today, there is a lot of sickness. Because of the food we have today, our people have diabetes, cancer, and heart problems.

The family unit is broken up. Today, no one can get along. Brothers and sisters are fighting. People are moving away from one another. A long time ago, everyone stayed together and helped each other. Everyone respected one another's belongings because it was great shame upon your family if one member were to take from another family. Today we have to use the padlock for security. Even padlocks don't work in some communities.

All of our ceremonies are about healing. If something is hurting you, you pray about it today and let it go. If you hold on to it inside, it will turn into a disease or energy that becomes ugly and will end up hurting people who are close to you. So, these are parts of our ways. But today you can't even trust the medicine People or ceremonies that were once the safest place to be. People call themselves medicine men very quickly. Once it took a lifetime to learn, but now it's all about money. We now have people that have a life of dysfunction suddenly change overnight and become medicine men. They overlook the teachings and protocols and become corrupt. They put price tags on ceremonies and they're doing more damage than good. The once-powerful Bundles now have keepers that have forgotten whom the Bundles belong to. They belong to our People, our children. Now we can't even trust people who walk the ceremonial path. It is a really difficult time we live in today.

When we talk about tradition and teaching, we talk through our stories. It is said that long ago our People lived in the Black Hills in caves. All these caves were connected. One day a young man came to the village. He was a powerful man, a fast and smooth talker. He spoke to the People in a powerful way. He told the People that if they went out of the caves above, there would be plenty of food and berries. He said that this place above was a paradise, a beautiful place. The People had a meeting, and decided to follow this leader. On top, they found out that there was food, but what he didn't tell them was that there were big animals called *oonk-c'-g'i-la* (dinosaurs). The People wanted to go back and they looked for this young man to lead them back, but he was nowhere to be found. They found out that this young man was an *ik-to-mi* (spider) or trickster and he had the power to change himself back and forth from an animal to a human. They say that in times in the future he will come back and trick the People. This is told today as part of our tradition. There are many *ik-to-mi* stories, funny stories that were taught by many of my grandparents.

I had many grandfathers and grandmothers. There was much laughter, but they were very strict. Everything was conducted in a circle. If you were late, they would make you walk all the way around the edge of the circle to the end and then you had to stand and pray to keep the energy calm and together. It was a strict culture. When a grandmother or grandfather spoke, everyone was quiet. You had no choice.

We say we are the caretakers of the heartbeat of Mother Earth, the caretakers of the heart. Every year, we gave offering of thanks to the Black Hills. With every heartbeat, a new life begins. The buffalo teachings gave us these things. We believe in the circle, the circle of life. We place ourselves in an imaginary circle. In a circle, everyone is equal. In the buffalo nation, everyone stands in a circle. Let's say someone has lost a loved one. From what we have witnessed in the buffalo nation, when one is down, they circle around, give their energy to the fallen one, and help them to stand. So it is the same with the People: We circle around, give them energy, and help them to carry on, help them to stand. We also replace the relative that has gone after one year, in order to heal the lost energy that the family was used to. Then the family does a *hun-ka* ceremony (adoption ceremony) to heal their family circle and from that time on, they are whole.

We recognize four stages of life. The first is the sacred child until the age of twelve. Then there is the coming of age ceremony, and that stage lasts until your twenties. The third stage is when you have earned everything; you earn your name. It is at the fourth stage when you become an elder. This is a never-ending cycle. When you become an elder, it should be a time when you have learned the cultural wisdom of everything. The People would listen to what you had to share and were not allowed to argue your thoughts. Today, when people get old, they say bad things and expect our People to listen, no matter what, because of that tradition. But the real truth is that those elders have not earned that knowledge. They have skipped over many teachings in our culture because of the changes society brought, so their words do not carry wisdom. Now their foolishness hurts people.

I would rather speak Lakota than English, because the language is more spiritual. There are many words that don't exist in our language. There are no foul words; there are no words to hurt people. The words themselves are based on food, medicine, and spiritual things. The words express feelings as part of the meaning. Lakota means "the people." The name Sioux is a French word meaning a snake in the grass. If the People today used their own language, there would be no harsh feelings. Traditionally, the words were like living in prayer. It was easier for different generations to speak, because of the very nature of our words.

No one had a hard time a long time ago. Everyone was connected. Everybody cared for each other. Your home was my home. Part of our tradition was humor, many jokes, and a lot of laughter. When an older elder would talk about something serious, he would throw in a joke to bring balance to what he was talking about. Even the Sundance ceremony, where everyone prayed for four days, created a lot of energy. Then there would be a *he-yo-ka* (a sacred clown), doing everything contrary and backward in order to bring in balance. It was in your everyday life. Children were always included in these ceremonies, even the very young. They just knew when to be quiet and not run around. Today, people look to babysitters before they go to pray.

The basic understanding as keepers of Mother Earth is our tradition. Some of our people are returning to our traditional ways. Part of that is our understanding of protocol. It is not just us, but all the First Nations. Our people were travelers. We roamed the country. We followed the buffalo by walking or riding horses. We never camped for long periods of time. We had to follow the buffalo for our food and learn from them. They were our brothers and we depended on them.

We believe in the cycle of life, where there is ending and no beginning. Teaching came from the animal nations. We have had the buffalo ceremony and horse ceremony since as far back as when our sacred White Buffalo Calf Bundle came. They were part of the instructions. We understood and respected the eagle and its knowledge, because it can fly the highest. We know that the eagle helps to see a long way, even into our future, and so they guide us. We never let an eagle feather fall to the ground. We always wear the feather high in our hair or on the staff. This is a sign of respect and honor.

We have an obligation to take care of our elders before they make the journey to the spirit world. We do not have a choice. To us, our elders are like gold. They are our wisdom-keepers. They are like living books. The sadness of today is that our elders from previous generations are different, because as young people they were sent off to boarding schools, so they missed all the guidance of coming of age and knowing the strength and spirit of earning a name. This all happened in the late 1800s after the massacres of our people. It was sad because we were all put on reservations also known as prison camps. Children as young as four or five were shipped off in order to break up the culture and our life-guiding traditions. Today's elders can't speak the language. So from that time we have seen a lot of changes. The elders never Sundanced or learned the importance of our ceremonies. In the boarding school era, there was a saying, "Kill the Indian and save the man." Our ways were outlawed. From that time to this, our ways were disrespected. Maybe that's why people don't respect the elders today. The kids today are very smart in ways that don't include the spirit of the earth; they know how to use the modern things. What they are lacking is the spiritual foundation, and that's very dangerous. They don't know their boundaries, so they seem to cross deadly boundaries that make them end up in prison, sometimes for life. They are out of balance.

Mother Earth is going to bring us back into balance. It's going to take disasters to make people humble and pray.

We are not prepared. I hear this from other Nations. A leader (an elder) is someone who thinks about the seventh generation, but today's leader only thinks about now and his pockets. Leaders long ago had to earn that leadership. Today, they become a leader overnight. Voted in. They create the votes by being liars or cheaters. Politics and spirituality don't come together. In modern times, it's whoever is most vocal and can speak for many that has power. They usually take the natural way of life for granted.

Mi-ta-ku-ye O-ya-sin means everything is related. Mother Earth is sick. There are many wise leaders who need to be heard, but many do not have the kind of voice that can be loud as today's leaders have, so loud it can hurt the ears. It is not real to make words that hurt Mother Earth. We need leaders who can be real, who will leave the beauty of Mother Earth for tomorrow's generations.

PART TWO

The Journey

Silent Secrets

I GUESS I HAD AN EPIPHANY, yet it wasn't an intuitive leap of understanding. It was more like a lightbulb on a dimmer that slowly illuminated the room, a rheostatted revelation. What I learned from the collective spirit of the oldest elders on this planet was not the result of a single event but of three years of accumulated interactions with them. I realized that these unique elders, who represented the oldest citizens of our collective culture, carried within themselves the full range of wisdom drawn from their life experiences. I set out to reveal these silent secrets.

My travels included both emotional highs and lows. While writing this book, a number of people whom I photographed passed away. It was a reality that began to color this project and attune my thoughts to what became a race against time. Unaccustomed to facing the fragility of life, I was introduced to the immediacy of death firsthand. I spent two months preparing to go to Australia, debating about the best way to travel; the last survivor of Gallipoli died while I dallied. There were two other incidents that stick in my mind, where death loitered near me as I photographed. I was in my hotel room in Amsterdam, gathering my equipment to drive near Brussels to photograph the oldest man in the Netherlands. For two months I had spoken to his son to arrange for permission. The father, Jan Bos, had been a national celebrity, initially rejecting the idea of another interview and all the fuss, but he finally agreed. I called just before leaving the hotel to say I was on my way. The phone rang many times and a solemn voice answered. The son told me his father had passed away less than an hour before. He was so sorry that I had traveled all this way for nothing. He apologized to me. To me? I was so saddened that I had interrupted this man's grief, I barely knew what to say.

Similarly, months before, while I was driving across the flatlands of the American prairie, musing about the interview and the photographs I had just taken and how I would crop the pictures, my cell phone rang. It was the director of the care facility I had just left, to let me know that Minnie Davidson had died. Minnie had seemed so distant, struggling to smile, and in hindsight, I wonder whether she may have been holding on to life for me that day. Again, I was saddened by the news and jarred by the proximity of death. I was just shocked by the nearness of the end for some of the people I was photographing. It became clear to me when I met these supercentenarians that at their advanced ages they had only a few years or months ahead of them. While family members, friends, and I wished for them to live on, to inspire and to share their insights, these seniors were comfortable with, and in some cases looking forward to, closing their eyes for the last time. It seemed a common trait, this sense of calm and feeling at peace with the way they had lived.

I became aware that this unique group of earth's eldest statesmen was virtually a hidden tribe. In many cases, only a few people in their remote villages or towns were privy to the details of their remarkable lives. To their descendents, they were family treasures, windows into the past, but I soon realized that their personal histories were of value to all of us. Their wisdom and legacy should be recorded. Their stories were lessons too valuable to be forgotten.

I can remember the delight of one niece, herself in her late seventies, brimming with pride over the knowledge that her aunt, then 114, was the oldest person on earth, and could recount stories of life in New York City as an emigrant in the late 1800s. To the niece, her aunt was just Aunt Charlotte, a kind woman who took care of her one-hundred-year-old sister, Tilley. To me, Charlotte Benkner was that and more, a part of the aging puzzle I had stumbled upon. She was also a kind of Rosetta stone for both science and sociology. A few demographers and a handful of geneticists around the world knew about her. Science wanted to unlock the secrets of her DNA, and discover which gene or set of genes she carried from her family that allowed her to reach the outer limits of extreme age. Geneticists had discovered her whereabouts. What was unavailable to the public was her life story. What factors external to her gene pool made it possible for Charlotte to live a long and healthy life? Charlotte was not alone in her isolation from view. Most of the people interviewed for this book lived behind our social "Iron Curtain." One-hundred-eleven-year-old Gladys Swetland lived in a hospital in a small town in the Allegheny Mountains; Joan Moll Riudavets, at 114, lived on a rather inaccessible island off the coast of Spain; and most of the other supercentenarians I interviewed were all but obscured from public view. As I began to build a macro view of all these people, I realized that most shared common experiences and held many of the same personality traits that seemed to protect both their mental and physical well-being. These people are the healthiest of the vigorous old, the tiniest percentage of the world's population. They potentially hold many of the answers to humankind's overriding desire to live as long as possible, free of many of the debilitating diseases that reduce our health. Increasingly, I felt an urgent need to grab this rare opportunity to bring their rich stories to light.

The proportion of the elderly population of the United States, as well as that of most advanced cultures around the world, has been increasing for decades. In the early part of this new century, the demographics of an aging population coupled with global pressures propelled health-related issues and aging to the forefront of topical discussion. The metaphor of the U.S. population as an hourglass, with aging baby boomers filling in the top section, the next generation at the narrow part of the glass, and their children at the bottom, graphically depicts and predicts an imbalance. Another graphic presents the population of the Western world as an inverted pyramid, with a broad aging population at the top supported by a narrowing base balanced on a point. These graphic examples will be both sobering to baby boomers and challenging to all individuals of the global community.

I felt that the tempo of my work became dictated by the inevitable pressure of time. I realized that I couldn't, and shouldn't, wait for a convenient time in my schedule to photograph these supercentenarians, as they were vanishing right in front of me. Years ago, I read that many of the cures for the diseases that plague humankind could be found in the rain forests of the earth, but that the encroaching loggers and growing settlements would create a situation where the forests would be lost before the cures could be discovered. That pretty well sums up my feelings about these elders, these supercentenarians. I'd like to think that the insights to be drawn from them are a curative for us all, that if we see ourselves with the same clarity that the lens has provided for us to view this special group, perhaps we might offer ourselves an opportunity to reconsider our attitudes about aging and the elderly, to grow old with vigor and grace, and to leave a template of healthy attitudes for our children.

One's personality or, to extend the metaphor of photography, white light, is mostly seen as a whole. The tricky part is using the right prism to refract and separate the wavelengths into various colors that make up light. It is equally challenging to tease apart the various traits or threads of the supercentenarians and arrange them to form an awesome spectrum of their personalities in a most unique way. Listening to their stories and feeling the emotion and energy behind their words allowed me to identify a number of shared traits, to refract their colorful histories that have led them to their remarkable ages, and to reveal the qualities many of them had in common.

Sidestepping Through Life

Sidestepping Through Life

ONE OF THE FIRST THINGS I LEARNED from these supercentenarians was that they had been healthy most of their lives. Startling as it may seem, most had avoided the maladies of life that plague the rest of us. Fore the most part, they had not been previously diagnosed with life-threatening issues that they recovered from; most had never really gotten sick. Members of this group ranged from those who had avoided most of the major illnesses of life, to a few who had suffered from cancer forty years ago and recovered, to a man who represented the extreme, never having been sick in his life save an occasional cold, and never having even been in the presence of a doctor.

Of the fifty-five people I have photographed to date, only ten were men, supporting the popular perception that women outlive men. With their life's work traditionally in the home, women avoided the hazards of the workplace and war. It is also possible that women are protected hormonally through estrogen, whereas men incur more health risks from testosterone. Was it possible that through these people science could answer questions that we have been seeking for ages? The answer is yes and no. While the medical world perhaps will never be able to study this particular group of supercentenarians at close range, research with younger centenarians is closing in on a number of resolutions, especially answers that indicate the importance of genes in inoculating us against some negative forces of aging.

The question re-emerges: Is the key to longevity lifestyle or genetics? While my observations are by no means a systematic study, my anecdotal observations of this unique group offer some points for reflection, and indicate certain threads, traits, actions, and thoughts common to these supercentenarians that are valuable learning tools for our own lifestyle choices

Optimism

T HE FIRST TRAIT that seems inextricably bound to the others is a positive attitude. It seems pretty basic, yet attitude impacts all aspects of life and is so
fundamental to this group. As I assembled my notes, the ideas from several
authors helped to shed light on why certain traits, including a positive attitude, were
so pervasive in supercentarians.

Let's start with a basic supposition that life is difficult and that the longer you live,
the more opportunity there is to encounter setbacks. During their upbringing, all of
these elders were presented with issues that we would find hard to fathom today.
Nature challenged their very existence. Heat, blizzards, disease, wars, famine, and
discrimination were the common words to describe events that threatened them
during their formative years. Yet, their remembrances were mainly that they were
undaunted. Martin Seligman, Ph.D., seems to explain this phenomenon in his book
Learned Optimism: "Finding temporary and specific causes for misfortune was the art
of hope."

Whether they grew up on the plains of America in the 1890s or in a village of huts
in Japan, few elders, if any, had the option when faced with adversity of giving up, or
choose another alternative, so they learned to persevere and overcome. Most would

tell me that their childhood was filled with wonderful memories, and only when pressed would they would say how harsh and difficult their day-to-day existence truly was. Seligman writes: "Our psychological health is something over which we have far greater control than we probably suspect. People who make universal explanations for [their] failures give up on everything when a failure spikes in one area. People who make specific explanations may become helpless in that one part of their lives yet march stalwartly on in other areas." I got the impression that to the supercentenarians, the hurdles of life were discrete challenges to overcome and that they were not to be overwhelmed by them.

Such was the case for Swami Bua, who was severely physically afflicted as a small child; Linus Reinhart, who at the age of thirteen became head of his family; Agnes Rich, who was born in a sod-house on the prairie; or Mitoyo Kawate, who lived through the horror of Hiroshima. Each of them isolated difficult experiences and focused on the bigger picture of life in positive terms. Their outlook on life seemed to support them during trying times and allow them to sidestep situations that would overwhelm most people. Zorba Paster, M.D., in his book *Longevity Code*, addresses this point. "Does our attitude truly have an impact on the length and sweetness of our lives? You bet it does. A negative, self-blaming, fatalistic attitude can end our lives prematurely. Our thoughts are powerful—perhaps not powerful enough to replace surgery for appendicitis, but certainly enough to lift some depression, stabilize blood pressure levels, and even bring cholesterol levels down. Conversely, they [negative attitudes] can also trigger anxiety, exacerbate depression, precipitate anger." Throughout my three-year journey spent witnessing these supercentenarians first-hand, I found that a constant among them was their ability to cope and adapt with a positive energy. Today, Lance Armstrong is celebrated for his tenacious attitude toward healing himself, a passion that supported his immune system to help overcome disease. Tomorrow, some of these elders may be recognized as heroes too.

Our Genetic Itinerary

WHEN ASKED ABOUT HER LONGEVITY, Emma Verona Johnston expressed, "Be careful about choosing your parents. Make sure they have good genes." Her humor was intact at 112 and so was the prescience of her thinking. Along with all of the other milestones in their lives, the supercentenarians have lived through the birth of advanced DNA sequencing, the basic principles of mitochondrial genetics, and the completion of the Human Genome Project. Time after time, when asked about long life in their families, the supercentarians would share, "My mother died at one hundred" or "My sister is ninety-seven" or, in the case of Juan Moll Riudavets, "I have brothers one hundred and nine and one hundred and four-years old who are still living." It's hard to deny the importance of genes in this group of supercentenarians. Genes are fundamental in predisposing some people to disease and others to health.

The complexity and challenge of the issues surrounding genetics, coupled with the myriad of historical and cultural biases we all bring to the discussion, drew me into the debate of nature versus nurture. I readily confess that I have a bias toward nurture, perhaps influenced by my hope that we have some ability to choose and change our destinies. It's through the nurture lens that I saw the supercentenarians.

Yet, science uses its own lens, the electron microscope, to make its case. Geneticists are beginning to understand that the slightest variance in normal chromosomal coding can cause disruptions in our lives, either causing debilitating disorders over which we presently have no control or, conversely, expressing a certain protein for protection. The human genome has been unlocked, and emphasis is being placed on studies to discover the magic this or the blockbuster that.

The origin of life required an environment within which an assortment of molecules had one crucial property: the ability to catalyze reactions that led, directly or indirectly, to production of other molecules that catalyzed themselves. From this all living creatures were formed, from the single cell to higher organisms such as ourselves, like cellular cities in which groups of cells perform specialized functions and are linked by intricate systems of communications. We communicate within emotional or physical environments like our cells and require nurturing surroundings to function properly. In his book *Mapping Human History,* Steve Olson points out that regarding "the intricate links between genes and experience, no one can say with certainty that a particular cognitive trait is, say, is fifty percent environmental and fifty percent genetic. The two are so intertwined that they cannot be separated. Even if a particular trait were found to be genetically influenced in a particular environment, that would say nothing about the genetic influence on that trait in other environments."

In the December 13, 2004, *New York Times* op-ed piece "The Behavior of Genes," Gene Robins wrote: "What these studies show is that the genome is responsive over different scales of time. These differences evolve over very long periods of time, from generation to generation. This is nature. Individuals may also differ in gene activity because of variations in their environment. This is nurture. But as much as people like to divide themselves into nature or nurture camps, what genes actually do in the brain reflects the interaction between hereditary and environmental information." There is ample scientific information to support the position that DNA contains the instructions for life (and death) and that this inherited template controls perhaps even our emotions. But that's not the whole story. It is the interaction with the environment that our genes inhabit that ultimately presages the outcome of well-being."

Coping and Adapting

A T SOME POINT IN THE LIVES of each of the elders, they faced physical or emotional trauma that tested their ability to cope. Their fundamental resiliency and positive spirit gave them the strength they needed to overcome tremendous challenges and adapt themselves to a new way of life. It was not always easy for me to separate out all the traits that had enabled these individuals to survive their "trials by fire," but it became clear that each of the oldest people on earth had triumphed over some form of enormous adversity. By Darwinian standards, they had developed the crucial survival skill: the instinctual ability to reinvent themselves or to modify their lives. While a handful seemed to have had an easier time than the rest of the supercentenarians, no one skated through life. Some hardships were emotional, some physical, and most were both.

Born without means, Pearl Gartrell picked cotton until her hands bled; ran the gauntlet of Southern segregation in the early 1900s; lost brothers, her father, and her husband at the hands of irrational cruelty; coped over and over to get through life—and she did it with a smile. As a small child, Damchaagin Gendendarjaa saw his monastery destroyed, watched his fellow monks sent to Siberia or killed in Mongolia, and went into hiding as a farmer to disappear from view and escape death. Almost sixty years later, he emerged after the fall of Communism to return to monastic life and become the lama of the Temple of Gandan.

Catarina Carreiro of Portugal witnessed her children starving and lived through four wars with meager food, yet maintained her equilibrium for herself and for the sake of her family. Each of them seemed to have preserved balance in their lives by being able to compartmentalize events, isolate traumas, and move on with their lives.

Values of Family

ONE OF THE FACTORS that seems key to an individual's longevity is the presence of a strong familial bond or support system of friends. A family support system gives those in the elderly population an advantage over other seniors who are isolated, lonely, and often depressed. Most of the supercentenarians I met were part of a close-knit community of family and/or friends. In particular, those who interacted with younger generations felt engaged in the world and experienced an enhanced sense of self-worth and well-being. Over and over, the biographies retold the histories of large families that stayed closely knit, in which the subsequent generations remained connected with the elders of the family.

The culture of the families and the societal norms included a reverence for the elderly that nurtured them in their senior years. Kamato Hongo, just shy of 116 and at the time the oldest person in the world, lived amongst four generations of her family. Watching and listening to them at home, I could see both the importance given to Kamato as well as the enjoyment each generation seemed to draw from her smile, her laughter, her songs. I watched her great-granddaughter hug her after coming home from school, grab her hand, tell her about the day, then scurry off to play. I don't doubt that the health of the whole family was advanced by the connection and support of one other. In other Japanese families I met, it was the rule, not the exception, that the grandparents lived with their children and grandchildren, even when daily medical assistance was needed.

Most, if not all, of the members of this supercentenarian group came from families of many children, not uncommon a century ago, where, as part of a collective, the needs of each individual were subordinate to the welfare of the group and each family member understood that a positive attitude was an asset to the group's positive functioning. The group in some ways functioned as a kitchen, nurturing and nourishing each individual. Social interactions stimulate active involvement in life. People sharing a vision demonstrate hopefulness as they move through life's challenges and obstacles together. And when multiple generations interact in the same environment, lifelong learning takes place between the young and the old.

Unlike the question raised by the chicken and the egg, it is clear which came first for these supercentenarians. They grew up in families where the larger entity—the family, the village, their faith—transcended personal issues. As a result, their lives had a purpose beyond their own individual needs, and each drew their strength from the links with others.

Longevity Is Color-Blind

Longevity is Color-Blind

AFTER CRISSCROSSING THE WORLD, locating supercentenarians on several continents, I was struck by the notion that the only reason that I could identify these supercentenarians was because their societies were structured to keep verifiable records. As an example, I was unable to travel to the continents of Africa and South America, not because there wasn't the potential for someone to reach age 110, but that the nations of these continents didn't keep accurate birth records. Many of the supercentenarians in the Deep South of this country were African-American, evidence that if there were precise record keepers from Togo or Mali, Africa would have been a fruitful continent for exploration of the very old as well. The Japanese, the Mongolians, Europeans, North Africans, and North Americans, both black and white, were all part of this exclusive club, given membership and included by age and not by skin color.

Over time there may be others discovered and validated in China or Eastern Europe, although again these verifiable records need to survive the chaos of history. My guess is that many cultures, as a result of structure and upheaval, have inadvertently excluded some of their population from recognition. Medicine maintains that, statistically, the poor and undereducated run a higher risk of suffering health risks, yet my experience has been the opposite. Generally poor and poorly educated, most of the supercentenarians defied these statistics. Perhaps there are other parts of the longevity mosaic that compensated the supercentenarians for the poverty and the lack of education they endured, fortifying them against natural health risks and ensuring their survival. For now, we can only speculate.

Hard Work

WE HAVE EVOLVED from a world of hunters and gatherers, a time in our history when we worked off 70 percent of our calories by foraging and hunting, to a society that could be described as a couch culture, where many of our calories are burned getting in and out of our cars. However, most if not all of the supercentenarians during the second part of the industrial revolution were born in rural areas where the livelihood of the family depended to a large degree on the labor of the children. Waking up at 5:30 a.m. to help with chores, often walking miles to school, then returning to do farmwork in the afternoons with homework done at night was a common routine. Before the advent of labor-saving inventions and the transportation revolution, all of these elders were engaged in lots of physical activity. "Working out" was not a scheduled event; it was a description of living. I was surprised to learn that many of these people chose to live labor-intensive lives well into their late nineties and early hundreds. I suspect some did it out of habit, but I would rather believe it simply made them feel good.

The simple rhythm of daily routines may also be seen as they had physical, often repetitive jobs that were calmative in their redundancy. The elders spent most of their time connected to nature, a connection that gave them context and a feeling of belonging to a higher order that they understood, even in the face of nature's unpredictable patterns. By extension, they were linked to plants and animals, to a rhythm as part of a daily routine in rural areas. Today a close relationship with nature is recognized as a therapeutic aid to stress by helping to lower blood pressure. Physical work throughout their lives seems to be a forecaster of longevity within this group of supercentenarians. Examples were everywhere. Fred Hale shoveled snow off his roof at 107, and Mitoyo Kowate farmed by herself until she was 99. Moses Hardy farmed into his eighties and then worked at his church until he was one hundred. There have been studies to support the view that exercise made them feel better about themselves.

The Harvard Alumni study, the Nurses Health study, the Framingham study, and many others have shown that those who exercise live longer than those who don't. Like our ancestors, I suspect that this group of supercentenarians were physically similar in that they were lean, muscular, and always active. One need only think of how much lifting, bending, walking, and climbing we do every day, in contrast to these oldest people. Being physically fit seems to be a predictor of longevity.

Eating

W HEN I INTERVIEWED PEOPLE FOR THIS BOOK, I would often ask about their eating habits over the course of their lives. I'd hear from them or their relatives about how, even in the Depression, there was always enough food to go around but not much more. When I was in Asia, I began to recognize a pattern of eating among the Japanese that was similar to the eating habits of supercentenarians in other parts in the world.

We all realize that we must eat to live. Unlike these supercentenarians, we have to make choices today from a vast food landscape that they never had in their youth, or for that matter throughout most of their lives. By percentage of population and as a percentage of the supercentenarians I've photographed, Japan has the largest group of the oldest people on earth. Taking a quick look at their diet, it is comprised of grains, fish, soy, fresh vegetables, very little meat, very little if any dairy products, and small portion sizes. Most of the older generations in Japan drink green tea regularly. Kamato Hongo and Shigechiyo Izumi, almost 116 and 120 respectively, came from the same village and were recognized as the oldest people in the world during their lifetimes. They drank a regional dark green tea revered for its medicinal properties. It was traditional for family members to eat, not at separate times, but at multigenerational tables with slow food (in contrast to today's fast foods), eaten slowly. If one can draw a conclusion from their stories, the supercentenarians grew up with family-style eating, where mealtimes provided opportunities for instruction and modeling of habits. The family was brought together at the table, to communicate and share. In Mongolia, I experienced the Ger, the traditional housing, a large tent-like structure where all generations lived and ate together in the round.

In Mongolia, when the story of the lama's personal eating bowl was told, it dawned on me that all of these extraordinary elderly people had similar eating habits that involved not just what they ate, but how they ate.

The lama, like most of his countrymen, always carried a silver-rimmed bowl, which hung from his belt. This bowl was given to him as a child and he would keep it throughout his life. The traditional way of cleaning the bowl after a meal was to lightly grind the edge on a stone. Over the years, as one grew older, the rim would wear away. There was wisdom inherent in the way this bowl was used. By accepting only what would fit into it as his meal, the lama would be sure not to overeat. As he aged, the bowl would grow smaller, as if to signal that he needed less food to sustain himself.

Another feature of diet that was pointed out to me by a farmer in Tennessee was that all of the supercentenarians, including his grandmother, grew up eating food that is today defined as "organic." There were no additives, no engineered ingredients, and no chemicals applied to the soil a century ago and as a consequence, these people matured without pesticide residue in their food or in their bodies.

Faith

IN A COZY LIVING ROOM in Jacksonville, Florida, I met Lena Dionne, who sat
with her priest while I took her portrait; in Northern Holland I listened to the son
of Sara van Grondelle-Bloom describe how he still takes his 112-year-old mother
to church every day; and I talked with the Lama Gendendarjaa of Mongolia, who,
at 110, spent the better part of the day in prayer. It didn't take long to figure out that
religion, faith, spirituality, whatever word fits your paradigm, was one of the key
components in the lives of all the supercentenarians. Certainly, some were more
religiously devout than others. Some were spiritually moved, while others pointed to
a general faith in a higher being or order. Each spiritual belief had its own shading,
but nonetheless they all gave context to the elders' lives.

The value of faith is no longer a matter of faith. It has been shown to improve the
immune system. Studies at medical schools around the world have findings to support the importance of faith in health and healing. Dr. Herbert Benson of Harvard, a
cardiologist by training, has spent the last thirty years researching and teaching how
personal beliefs influence health and well-being in the mind-body connection. Most
of the supercentenarians knew much of this intuitively and embraced spirituality as

a cornerstone of their longevity. From Mississippi to Mongolia, spirituality as an essential part of their lives repeated itself in almost every conversation I had.

Miracles, moral daily conduct, willing yourself to cure, managing the stress of life; these are but a few of the concepts of faith. Each group defines it differently, or uses different words to explain the same issues, but underlying all of this is the powerful force of community that sprung from faith and spread a wide net that nurtured the elders and buffered them from many of the shocks that they endured living through three centuries. Each time I photographed someone I would ask the question, "So tell me, can you let me in on your secret? Why do you think you have gotten to be this old?" " The Lord," they would say, almost each and every time.

Rural Life

ON A CLEAR DAY, they could always see an open field, a mountain, the sea, or a forest. Without the haze of electric light they could always look at the night sky sparkling with stars.

Almost to a person, each supercentenarian grew up encircled by nature in a rural environment. It seems to me that in the race to reveal which gene or combination of genes produced an immune system to enable these unique people to outlive the rest of the planet, not enough recognition is given to the importance of their early environment. Henry David Thoreau spoke of the notion that man may be seen as "part and parcel of Nature, rather than [as] a member of society."

Granted, in the 1890s, a large part of the population was still involved in agriculture, but a migration to the cities had already begun. While urban areas were growing and attracting people, this group of elders remained in the country for the better part of their lives. The rhythm and scope and perhaps the unattainable understanding of nature gave each person a context to live within, and offered simple answers to physical, emotional, and spiritual questions. Nature shows us that we are not alone but part of a bigger system which often dictates our daily cadence. Running concurrently with this rural scene was the pattern of being disadvantaged, at least by today's standards. From a distance, this limitation may have become a positive advantage in longevity in promoting many of the other silent secrets of the group. From the elders themselves I heard descriptions of their lives woven with stories of woods and fields, of fishing on rivers and lakes, of walking and riding horses, of one-room schoolhouses and Saturday-night dances at the church. I don't wish to romanticize "the old days" too much, but I do recognize that the rural framework of the supercentenarians rewarded them with simple happiness. Repeatedly, I heard it said, "We were poor but we always had enough and we were happy." They expressed a level of contentment that I admired. They spoke of their humble beginnings not with regret or shame but with a sense of honor.

Humor

A GRANDSON TOLD ME about his grandmother's humor, which was famous in the family and remained intact at 113 years of age. "Grandma Lizzie?" he said. "Did you miss me, I haven't seen you for a while. "Miss you?" she replied. "You don't come around enough for me to miss you." Think about this statement. Grandma Lizzie used wit, a cognitive element, and mirth, an emotional element, both parts of humor, to deal with annoyance in a positive way. Happiness, and by connection health, seemed to be a chuckle away.

While a few of the supercentenarians cracked jokes, and I witnessed some laughing at their own jokes, most of their family members and some of the supercentenarians characterized themselves as always being able to see the funny side of life. I realized after a number of interviews that a sense of humor was one of the assets that bolstered their longevity. I had never thought much of humor in this context, as a way to sustain our immune system, and I needed to understand the research that was being conducted. Humor is now a serious topic in behavioral medicine. As psychologist Steven Sultanoff put it, "Therapeutic humor is more than a discrete moment in time. It is not a joke, anecdote, or funny situation. Instead, it is a perspective or way of being in the world—a way of enjoying the ups and downs of life."

Coupled with the supercentenarians' coping skills, humor seems to have played a part in the mind-body connection over the years and was present even at their advanced ages. Kathleen Gregson chuckled to herself and made me laugh, and so did Bettie Wilson. Joan Moll Riudavets made me laugh. Susie Gibson laughed at me. Pearl Gartrell, a courageous woman who has endured more than most, still chuckled and shook her head at life when recounting her stories. Her humor, and other coping attitudes, bubble-wrapped her emotions or helped reverse the stress caused by the wounds of segregation.

The Package

THE ELDERS OF THE EARTH should serve as reminders that we need not surrender our health and often our happiness to the vagaries of age. While I may sound like some self-help guru chiding his readers to "take charge of their lives," I honestly believe that many of the practical lessons learned from these supercentenarians can have a significant, positive impact on health and well-being. I have formed a number of opinions from the interviews of these supercentenarians that I have felt the need to share. Each time I interviewed, I was forced to shift focus from the last person I had photographed to the new person in frame; and yet, with fresh eyes and a fresh perspective, the images revealed a commonality. I have identified threads woven through their lives that are exclusive of genes. These traits may act as switches to turn genes on and off.

The Shangri-la Effect

The Shangri-la Effect

I OBSERVED that almost to the person, the supercentenarians looked younger than their biological ages. Some, astoundingly, looked twenty to thirty years younger. Whether it was the quality of their skin, their vibrancy, or the energy in their smiles, time seems to have marked its increments more slowly with this group than the rest of us. They seem to have been inoculated by their behavior and their genes, and to have developed both an immune system far beyond the norm and a means of slowing down the inevitable maturing of their cells.

I am surprised by my observations. I went off looking for portraits and wound up finding pieces to a puzzle. This odyssey didn't reveal some fountain of youth, or a special herb eaten by all, but the overwhelming common sense that binds the threads together. If there is something unique to the theme of this book, it's that this complex mosaic of traits can't easily be cherry-picked, but individually each is attainable. If you want to apply these guidelines to your life, be aware that the successful aging of the supercentenarians has required all of the traits be present, forming a living-code perhaps even unconsciously. We would like to find something—a pill, a chant, that one exercise or special diet—that would give us that edge for health and longevity. We want it easy and we want it fast. The simple answer is, it's the package. It's difficult to assemble and it takes a lifetime.

I've tackled something that is usually left to the domain of academicians, social scientists, and psychologists. Had I not stumbled across this unique group of people, I would have continued to embrace my generation's myopic views of the elderly. I feel fortunate, and I believe now somewhat qualified, having met and interviewed so many of the oldest people on earth, to comment and draw very personal conclusions without a background of scientific methodology. Perhaps a more academic approach would have been helpful, or then again, it may have been an encumbrance; I'll never know. This is in no way an apology, or a disclaimer, just an honest appraisal of my strengths and limitations in sharing my experiences.

PART THREE

The Elders

MRS. SMITH WAS THE FIRST PERSON I PHOTOGRAPHED for this project. I realize in hindsight that my long journey began with her and what she taught me that crisp morning in Manchester-by-the-Sea would ultimately change all of my preconceived ideas about what this project would be. I started by approaching Mrs. Smith as I had done countless other advertising assignments, with a carload of equipment, an assistant, a shooting schedule, trying to impose order on the individual and framing the final image in my mind before the first photograph was taken. What was I thinking? I learned a lot that day about needing to travel light, and more important, how I tended to come up short in the sensitivity department. I, like most, had never spent much time around "old people," perhaps out of a fear that mortality might be catching. All that changed with time. Mrs. Ann Smith was my first test.

She was living in a retirement home on the north shore of Massachusetts in an imposing old house overlooking the sea. I set up a backdrop in a grand living room of the facility and waited for her to finish eating before starting to take her portrait. The sounds, the smells, the pace of the retirement home were all new to me. As I began to photograph her, I realized how ill-prepared I was to talk with her; my own fumbling for words and not knowing what questions to ask or how to ask them embarrassed me. Mrs. Smith (I couldn't call her by her first name because she was double my age and it made me feel uncomfortable) sensed this and didn't make things easier. The result was a set of good contact sheets and very little information. It was to her daughter Helen that I had to turn to learn about the life of Ann Smith.

Mrs. Smith was born in Latrobe, Pennsylvania, one of four children, whose family moved frequently as her father traveled to different cities to set up steel mills. When she was small her family moved to Chicago. She somehow spent a few years "back East" with her two aunts on Cape Cod who had no children. The family moved to New Jersey later and Mrs. Smith went on to Teachers College in Perth Amboy, New Jersey. She taught most of her life in one form or another. When she was in her seventies she volunteered to teach at a Civilian Conservation Camp to teach basic skills to undereducated men. Giving to others was a way of life for her.

One of Ann Smith's clearest early recollections was of being a young girl and seeing Teddy Roosevelt campaigning from the back of a train. She lived through the First World War and then the flu pandemic of 1918. She volunteered to work in the flu wards, as she didn't seem to be susceptible to the disease. In fact, throughout her life she was basically free of sickness until the age of 105 when she fell and broke her hip.

She shouldered a lot of responsibility, often acting as head of the household when the men were at war. She had a burning Protestant faith that guided her, a faith that directed her to work hard and give to others. She always took in other members of her family and made room for them at the dinner table.

During the Depression the family was never for want of food as she grew lettuces, peas, beans, and potatoes in her vegetable garden, had access to fish from the ocean, and made sure that healthy food was served. Her daughter said that her mother prayed every night before bed, her coping mechanism for the next day.

I looked at the images a few days after the shooting and hadn't yet realized what I had stumbled upon. Underneath the façade of this frail woman in a wheelchair were three centuries of history; a teacher, literally, waiting with her life-lessons plan to begin my studies; like any archeologist, I had just begun to scratch the surface.

1890

Fred Hale

Born December 1, 1890
New Sharon, Maine
U.S.A.

FRED HALE SENIOR WAS THE SECOND SUPERCENTENARIAN I photographed for this project. I've had the privilege to speak with him and his family over the last few years. Many of my insights into the longevity of the supercemntenarians began with Fred's life stories and have been borne out by the other elders I've met. While there are clear signs that genetics and hereditary play a part in Fred's vibrancy, it is also my belief that his gestalt—his attitudes, his work ethic, his spirit—over which he had control has played an even greater role in his health.

I traveled to upstate New York, stayed in a motel by the interstate, and spent a little time the next morning at breakfast becoming acquainted with his son, eighty-year-old Fred Hale, Jr., at a local diner. I was told a little about Fred's life by his son but was advised I could get my questions answered by his father at the assisted living facility where he now lives. I just had to speak up a little for his father to hear. I felt nervous as I set up my equipment. Years of photographing ads for multimillion-dollar accounts did not help to calm me. I had never spent time interviewing people and this project meant a lot more to me than any business assignment. Or maybe I was aware that this was the biggest job of my career. Fred and his family couldn't have been more gracious. I concentrated on the viewfinder. I let his story take over.

If you wanted a voice-over that evoked the distinctive cadence of a New England accent, you couldn't have found a better voice than Fred's.

"I was born December 1, 1890, in New Sharon, Maine. Born on a small farm and lived there with my parents and brother. The house had a large kitchen and wood-burning stoves to heat the rooms. On 180 acres we raised corn, potatoes, beets and took the sheep to market for cash."

When I asked Fred what his earliest recollection was, he gave me a taste of his wry Maine humor. "Well, let's see, that was a while ago," he quipped with a bit of a grin. His earliest clear memory was the winter he was six, sitting in a sleigh covered by a thick blanket, drawn by two horses crossing a frozen river to go visiting.

"Didn't have any childhood friends . . .we lived two miles from the village and I had to work. There was little time for fun. I had to work," he repeated.

He did admit that his father let him go fishing on the brook that ran through the farm. Fred Sr. also recalled that his father either bought or made him a sled. " That's how I got acquainted with Fred Jr.'s mother . . .she borrowed the sled, she lived up on the hill and could slide all the way to the schoolyard." He could remember his father cutting blocks from a frozen lake and packing them in sawdust for ice in the summer. Fred's job as a young boy was to tend the lambs. The town butcher would come by the farm to slaughter them and then he and his father would take them down to Boston to sell. One hundred years later, he could still recollect that the lambs could not weigh more than twenty-eight pounds for marketing.

All seasons represented hard physical work. Whether cleaning the barns or haying the fields, exercise was an everyday aspect of Fred's life. It kept him healthy. He can't remember ever having taken a pill in his life. He described how it was, his job in the rough Maine winters, to maintain the roads.

"A team of horses would pull a large wooden roller to pack the snow on the roads for the sleighs. If there was a drift too big, I had to dig out the drift by hand to get through," he said. As he told me this story, I couldn't help but think how soft we've become.

"We got up early, did chores, went to bed," he said. "But Sundays, Sundays were a day of rest . . . they were quiet time to visit with my grandparents and talk." I asked if issues were discussed like events of the times, news of the day.

"Well, we had no radio, no papers . . . got all our information from the Saturday Evening Post each week . . . didn't know much about what was going on."

When he was twenty-seven, he became a railroad postal clerk, delivering mail on a daily run from Bangor to Boston. He would ride his bicycle to work, rain, snow, or sunshine, and that included nights. He would stand on the train behind the engineer and hook a mail pouch to a pole as the train would slow through a town. Fred still has a box of flash cards that he had memorized for postal addresses. He retired in 1957 after delivering mail for thirty-nine years. Today he is the oldest living postal worker in history.

"After he retired, he spent time hunting and fishing. Hunting with his sons and grandsons, it's always been on one of his greatest thrills," said his son. As a younger man, he would go off with his mail (it was his pun) buddies to hunt. He has also kept bees for many years. Fred swears that the reason he doesn't have arthritis at his age is that he's eaten a spoonful of bee pollen every day for forty years. Medicine is coming around to Fred's way of thinking. Scientists are currently investigating the therapeutic properties of bee pollen and the way bee venom stimulates our bodies' immune system. His son has started taking bee pollen too. Fred Jr. smiled, "If it works for him it should work for me." I figured I could also learn from Fred Sr.'s example and made a mental note to try it out.

Perhaps the most amusing story from Fred came about when he was 107 and still living on his own. At that age, he was the world's oldest licensed driver.

There had been a heavy snowfall in Maine and Fred was up on his porch roof shoveling off the snow. When he finished, he hopped off into a snow bank and then went into his house to change his wet clothes. Suddenly he noticed there were flashing lights outside. When he opened the door, there were the firemen and police who'd come to his rescue. When he was told that a passerby had seen someone fall off the roof, Fred quipped, "I didn't fall, I jumped!" and slammed the door.

Fred has been confined to a wheelchair and the assisted care facility after he tripped and broke his hip. That hasn't dulled his mind, however. He still jokes and plays cards with his son of eighty. He read a little and loved to watch the Red Sox. Clearly, he was the oldest Red Sox fan in the world. When asked why he had lived so long he jibed, " Oh, I don't know, punishment I guess. I've enjoyed all my years, each one. I even like the recent one."

Fred was the beginning of a process for me that hasn't stopped. After my encounter with him, he became an early benchmark for all the other supercentenarians I was to meet.

The last time we spoke I asked, "If there was one piece of wisdom you'd like to pass on to your grandchildren what would it be?"

"You have one life to live, live it well, and don't disgrace your family."

This funny, polite man has made me pause. He has made me think. He's also the reason I have bee pollen on my cereal.

John McMorran

Born June 19, 1889
Michigan, U.S.A.

L AKELAND, FLORIDA, WAS HOT and sticky in May. The wide highways leading to John McMorran were lined with drive-in everything, from liquor and food stores to pawnbrokers, churches, and funeral parlors. We live in a mobile culture. It is perhaps this same mobile country that has contributed to the dire circumstances of many of the aged. My first gloomy impression of this area where John McMorran resided lingered with me as I entered the care facility: a place with elderly citizens clustered in wheelchairs, going nowhere, and watching television. A wave of sadness took hold of me. I found John sitting slumped over in his wheelchair in the hallway. New to this retirement setting, to the sights, sounds, and smells, I couldn't tell if he was breathing. Maybe he died and no one knew? I found a nurse who yelled in his ear, "John, someone's here to see you," and he stirred. I had been anticipating another Fred Hale experience, another energetic, engaging man full of anecdotes. John McMorran was the oldest male in America at the time but he was clearly not the one in the best shape.

Most of the story surrounding his life came from news clippings and a bio given to me by the retirement home. John's grandparents came from Ireland in the 1840s. They purchased 120 wooded acres in Goodland Township in Michigan and they had to clear the land before farming. A log cabin was built and John's father, George, was born there. When George grew up he married the girl across the road and they rented an adjacent farm. John was born on June 19, 1889, and while growing up lived on a number of farms in the area. Not much is known about his childhood except that he had to walk one mile every day to the schoolhouse. At the age of twenty-four, he married Matie Leader, three years his senior, and they moved from town to town until

finally they bought a farm in Capac Michigan. One year later, John traded the farm for a truck and started hauling freight. Eventually, he hauled milk from Pt. Huron to Detroit until 1945. His wife, Matie, died in 1964 and John moved to Florida for the rest of his life.

I learned that John's parents died relatively young; his siblings, however, showed a genetic indicator of long life: his sisters died at 88, 103, and his brother at 83. Little is known of their lives. In addition, John possessed a lively sense of humor, another indicator of longevity. Recently he was asked at what age he had retired. He answered, "I'm not retired yet!"

While I was photographing John, I would ask him questions, many that I realized he did not hear. I left the area to find someone to speak with him. His "handler," an affable overworked woman, would speak directly into his ear. He would raise his head but would repeat, "I'm cold" or "leave me alone" and drop his chin again. There was a brief period when John responded to a joke, smiled as my camera clicked away, then stopped, looked away, and the session was over.

I sat in the parking lot with the steady stream of traffic behind me on the highway and this squeaky-clean retirement home in front of me. I was mulling over what I had just seen. I realized my education was just beginning. My stereotyped view of dignified old age was being tempered with John's reality, one that he shared with many seniors, of a lonely, mostly forgotten parent and grandparent living out the end of his or her life in a clean, antiseptic health care facility far from family. Don't get me wrong. The staff there seemed caring in the sense of parceling out bits of their concern spread among the residents. They were maintaining the residents but I'm not sure I'd call it living with any dignity. Collections of wheelchairs, like so many cars at a drive-in movie, were passive and parked. It was the general isolation that struck me, that got under my skin. They were in there and I was out here. The seeds of my future work had been sown.

Hazel Luther

Born December 11, 1889
Worcester, Massachusetts
U.S.A.

FLORIDA WAS ALREADY HOT and steamy late in May. I had no trouble finding the low, unassuming building of the Olds Hall Good Samaritan Center on a back street in Daytona. Brimming with plants and birds in the entryway, this Lutheran care-facility immediately gave me the feeling of being in someone's cheery and comfortable home. I was shown to the chapel to meet Hazel. As she greeted me, I was struck by the melody of her speech. A tiny, dignified woman with both lilt and laughter in her voice, she raised a frail hand of introduction as homage to etiquette. She spoke with clarity and immediately charmed me.

She was born in Worcester, Massachusetts, as Hazel Houghton Penniman, and a descendant of Pilgrims that arrived on the Mayflower. The daughter of a busy veterinarian, she could remember accompanying her father on his farm visits. She considered medicine as a vocation but in those days, few women became physicians so her parents steered her toward a more refined life of music. "Oh yes, I loved to dance and sing and play the piano." She entered the Institute of Musical Art, which later became the Julliard School of Music, where she studied voice, piano, music theory, German, and Italian. In her diary and personal papers provided by her great-niece, Hazel described the anxiety she felt during her first recital, being "scared green" and having "wobbly knees and parched lips." In 1916, she sang at a concert to honor Percy Grainger, a well-known composer of the time, and kept the program he autographed. She married in 1918, moved to Michigan, and began a long career of teaching music. Though she never had children, she referred to her students as her family.

After the age of one hundred, Hazel experienced several medical problems but I

was told she overcame these with her positive attitude. The Good Samaritan Center reported that she told a staff member that she grieved for another roommate who had passed away but that "there was nothing to be gained from dwelling on my grief."

While I photographed her, I asked her questions about her life. Her answers were always positive, upbeat. Music had been such a large part of her life. So too had been her religious faith. She was obviously happy and nurtured by those around her. It seemed also that her being there gave a special meaning to many of the staff. She was clearly nurturing them as well; I watched them stop, call her name or touch her hand, then go about their work. As I looked through the lens and spoke to her, mid-sentence she closed her eyes and fell quietly asleep. I stood back to take in the whole scene. In her beloved parlor, Hazel was peacefully napping in her chair while all around her, the birds were chirping in their cages while activity continued all around her.

At 112, this petite, demure woman seemed to be wrapped in her religious and musical convictions. At first, I didn't believe there really were people who thought this way, jaded as I was by the cynicism of a fast-paced cosmopolitan life. Hazel, by contrast, presented an image of a person completely content within herself. When I asked her why she thought she had reached such an advanced age, she simply looked heavenward and said, "Goodness, He knows." In her diary, she had copied down quotes that she used to guide her life. A 1915 entry read: "Music loosens a heart that care has bound." In another entry in the margin, she had written a definition of worry: "[It] comes from an Anglo Saxon verb to choke, that's just what it does to you. It's one of your worst enemies." On that steamy afternoon in May, Hazel Luther was living proof that one can battle against worry and live with a heart as light as song.

1888

Pearl Gartrell

Born April 1, 1888?
Tillsdale, Georgia
U.S.A.

I
T WAS NOT YET NINE O'CLOCK in the morning and the heat was rising out of the grass. I had found Pearl and her grandniece Lolita in a modest apartment in a rundown section of Jacksonville, Florida. The screen door hung from the hinge, children ran around playing between the buildings, and two girls played jump rope but cast a curious eye toward me, the white guy with a load of equipment.

Pearl was afraid to come out from behind the door. Her grandniece had to coax her into the room. Lolita whispered to me, "Granny's afraid of white people," but she came in nonetheless without a cane and sat there quietly, holding her picture of Jesus. "It's a pleasure to meet you," I said, offering to shake her hand. She nodded and only lightly touched my hand. Looking out into space and stroking her chin, as if traveling back in time, she began to answer my questions and her words began to flow.

Pearl Gartrell was born on a small farm in Georgia, one of the youngest of thirteen brothers and sisters. Pearl said in a slow, rich Georgia accent. "Mauma, she was a big woman n sit o the porch an wach us work." My ears strained to understand. Her house had been a wooden, unpainted structure up on bricks. "You could see the ground through them cracks" in the floorboards and the cold coming up in the winter. There was a single, deep cooking fireplace that served many functions." Peoples theyd come in, "remembering her parents blackening the children's faces with soot, telling them to be still and hiding them in the back of the fireplace when the Klu Klux Klan came to the house. Her father, husband, and two brothers were killed in this small town. Her mother was a midwife and worked for the local white doctor. At times, she dispensed herbal remedies to the family and neighbors. Pearl still doesn't believe in

doctors. When anyone in the family was "reel sick, Mauma workd off the payment in da house." "So were there any black doctors?" I said. "Dere was ds one he id a hole an put you in fo sa night, jus your head out... for lumbago. I didn't trus im." She chuckled and looked away so as not to look me in the eye.

Daily life was hard. The routine was to be up by dawn, do chores, and be off to a one-room schoolhouse attached to the Baptist church. She and the rest of the children would walk barefoot, carrying their shoes to school and putting them on before entering so as not to wear out the leather. School lasted only a few hours and then it was back to work at the farm. "Ida walks behind ar mules, to plough the fields for cotton and tobacco," Pearl said. Not so fondly, she remembered picking cotton until dark, her hands bleeding; she wasn't allowed to quit until she had filled her quota. She remembered the family vegetable plot. "We'd have mor' nough, we gave to those didn't hav. Evn gave hogs."

"Granny," Lolita asked, "what did you like to do?"

"Goin hunting for possum, coon, and rabbit," she replied.

To this day Pearl's 105-year-old sister still prefers possum for a meal. As a young black woman, the only nonfarming work that was available was as an "ironing maid" in the "white man's laundry." Segregation left its mark on her and she was taught to be submissive and to never talk back. Pearl had two children by "the white man in town" and when she heard the "white folks as com'n to get thim and drown 'em in a croaker sack in da river," she ran from Georgia.

Yet, in spite of all this, she retains a sense of humor. If you were to ask me why she's as old as she is it seems I guess there are many factors. A life of hard work, being fit and not overweight, eating simple foods, and having a deep-seated faith. Add to that a rare genetic component for aging slowly. When I asked her why she's lived as long as she has, she smiled and said because of Jesus and because she could cry. "Men don't cry, they hold it in," she said.

When I asked if anything through her life had worried her, knowing what kind of life she had lived, she said, "Worry? Worry ain't no good from worrying." "If there was one lesson to pass on to your grandchildren and others what would it be?" I asked. "Trus in da lord, he's a mighty man."

Then she smiled, an impish sort of smile, but she looked away. She walked to the screen door and peered out as I was leaving. She even waved goodbye to me.

Harriet McGhee

Born March 14, 1894
Leesburg, Georgia
U.S.A.

MOST OF THE INFORMATION that I learned about Harriet came from a great-grandniece. From Harriet, I learned about the caring that some people extend to others, even strangers.

I drove up to a small house at the end of a street lined with huge old trees that formed a canopy to shade the June heat. The red clay of the earth had been grooved by a history of wheels and the ruts steered me to the side of the house. This was a private residence that had been converted to form a group home; the ground floor had been reconfigured to accommodate six or seven seniors. I walked in through the back, entering a kitchen packed with large pots and immense mixing bowls and bustling with lunch preparation. While waiting to meet Harriet in the sitting room, I wandered out to the front porch. There, in a row of old wooden rocking chairs were four elderly people, all facing the road, taking in the sights as they fanned themselves in the steaming heat of the day. I asked them how things were; they were all so polite and charming. "Yesah, its a warm one," they nodded, smiling and rocking contentedly.

When I photographed Harriet McGhee in the small dining room of the house, she seemed so frail. Some of the people in the kitchen came in to see how she was doing, filling in some of the blanks to my questions before slipping back to the simmering pots in the next room. Harriet had cooked most of her life; for the last fifty years, before she moved to this house, she had worked at both a local school and at her church. She was a neat, proud woman who never asked for help from anyone. Thin, active, devout, she lived a life free of excess. What I sensed was that now she was part of a special "family," unrelated by blood but nonetheless bound together by this house. Their close community seemed to be surviving on a shoestring but succeeding by the strength of its spirit.

Harriet was born in Leesburg, Georgia, and may very well been the daughter of a former African-American slave. She grew up on a small farm where the family grew peanuts, cotton, and corn. She was married at fifteen and moved to Albany, Georgia, where she remained for the rest of her life.

As I was soon to learn, a number of the people that I was to photograph had simple lives. No sensational life stories, yet each imparted a small piece that added up to

a larger picture of what it means to achieve longevity and health. Here was a snapshot of health and mental hygiene, from a supercentenarians surrounded by a community of supportive seniors.

When I was finished and I pulled out of the driveway, I looked back at the porch. The group of four still sat there; they waved to me, and they smiled and they continued to rock. I don't know that it is possible to quantify the value of community as a component of health but the elders on porch spoke volumes on the subject. Science seems to want to take credit for many of the advances in health and longevity, but my vote is for the porch.

Liza Johnson

Born June 28, 1887
Buena Vista, Georgia
U.S.A.

I ARRIVED IN THE TOWN OF BUENA VISTA, GEORGIA, a little before noon and too early. I didn't want to disturb the lunchtime of Liza Johnson. Hot, tired, and cramped from a long drive on back roads, I parked in the main square and strolled around the town. My first impression was that time had stood still for a little while here. Parking on the diagonal without another car nearby or any demarcation lines or parking meters, my big-city consciousness was raised as I discovered how differently everything is arranged in a small town. I walked into the five-and- dime and stepped back into the era of Norman Rockwell. A twenty-five-foot-high tin ceiling hung over low rows of wooden counters of merchandise, bolts of cloth, jewelry, and food. A small soda counter and a magazine rack hugged the wall. The cashier said there was a restaurant in town, and walking across the square, I couldn't help but notice that there were few people on the street, a fact that explained why the restaurant was closed when I reached the door. I gave up the idea of eating. I nosed the car under the only overhead blinking traffic light, and drove down a long windy road to the nursing home on the outskirts of town.

I found the nursing home to be in stark contrast to the town. Instead of the eerie quiet of barren street, here there was a traffic jam of gurneys, wheelchairs, and walkers. Modern, clean, brightly lit, full of residents, nurses, and attendants; the thought crossed my mind that most of the town must live in here. Liza's closest relative lived in town and was supposed meet me at the nursing home but I was told she didn't have a way of getting there. I volunteered to pick her up but she didn't have a babysitter to watch her children, and I got the impression she really didn't want to come by, so I was left the learn about the life of Liza Johnson from Liza herself and from her nurse during the interview.

Miss Liza, as her caregiver referred to her, had a grip like a vise when I shook her hand. She had been made up for her portrait and seemed genuinely delighted with the attention and fuss that was being made about her. She was also a mischief-maker; she kept motioning for the nurse and me to get together, to stand next to each other while shaking her head and giggling. Liza may have been the first person that I met on this project that openly expressed her interest in continuing an active life, including an active sex life. Up until then I hadn't thought much about the sexual aspect of growing old. Naïve on my part. Sexuality is such a large part of one's existence, it stands to reason that in whatever form in manifests itself in later years, it's still important. Yet I confess I didn't pursue this topic with Liza. Or her nurse. I was looking for biographical information, stories of her youth, but her early life story was unfortunately more than a little sketchy. "Did you have brothers and sisters, Liza?" I asked. "Yup," was her answer. Her nurse told me Liza was born in Harris County, Georgia, and had seven brothers and sisters. "Did you have any children?" "Mmmm." she said. She'd had ten children but they all had died. "Was there anything you can remember from your life that was a high point, a funny story or even a sad story?" I asked, thinking the question would spark a memory. "Fishing," Liza replied. She had told the nurse that she loved to fish all her life and in fact had gone on a nursing home outing the previous week and caught a catfish. Liza seemed healthy and at her age, and who knows how many years she would live. I had hoped for some history from the nursing staff but no one had been there long enough to hear any of Liza's stories.

As I left the beautifully landscaped nursing home and headed back to the interstate, I stopped on the way to look at the town's small cemetery. It was neatly mowed and planted, with an ironic greeting for anyone bothering to stop: NO THRU TRAFFIC read the sign posted at the entrance.

I laughed at the thought but grew somber as I drove on. Liza was in the nursing home by herself, marking time, concealed from view, her family gone, with no meaningful contact with the outside world. The nurse and others of the staff seemed genuinely caring if a bit overwhelmed by the workload. Like so many elders in facilities all over the country, Liza wanted to cling to life, to embrace it with style and yet she spent her days in relative isolation. The nurse had said no one had visited her in quite a while; I had been the only "through traffic" in a long time.

Agnes Rich

Born January 20,1892
the prairie, Nebraska
U.S.A.

"I WAS BORN in a sod house on the prairie," said Agnes Rich, and she made me stop and think about what that really meant. With all the creature comforts of today, living in a sod house must have been like living in a cave. As I sat listening to Agnes's life story of her pioneer beginnings on the prairie, it seemed like something out of the pages of Willa Cather's *My Antonia*. She began her life with no alternatives. Unlike the Outward Bound experiences of today, where parents pay large sums of money to send their children into nature to develop self-esteem, self-reliance, and concern for others, Agnes, like the other supercentenarians, was born into these circumstances without choice. We pretend to know the way it was, we weekend camping warriors, but Agnes knew the way it was. She was a witness to a past that only a handful of people living today can share. Her father built a log cabin when he was able and by the time Agnes was eight, the family was ready to move.

In 1900, Agnes and her family went by wagon train from Nebraska across the plains to Texas. She saw the remnants of our Native Americans on her journey, and settled down on a small farm and began a new life. Along with her eight brothers and sisters, Agnes would rise at four in the morning to feed the chickens before school. After school, she would return to her chores until nightfall. Their lives were hard, dictated by the rhythm of farming. I often wonder if a simple life, free of the complexities of today's social and urban constructs, is not just a happier but also a healthier way to live.

Looking through the viewfinder, I saw a tall, thin woman with beautiful skin. What I heard from her were the words of a woman at peace with herself, a woman with dignity who could remember songs of her childhood and, with happiness, put the harshness of her early years into perspective. Maybe it was one of the gifts given to someone who has lived this long that she could recognize the unseen benefit in almost anything. It was a wonderful lesson to learn and it seemed all the more poignant coming from a woman 111 years old.

For Agnes, as with the other supercentenarians, there is no way to separate out the individual components of longevity and give them each a statistical weight. Genetics plays a role, but how much? Was Agnes's longevity attributable to her life of hard

work, or to the fact that she was a thin woman who never overate, or to her sense of humor that her family spoke about, or to a bunch of genes that she carries that we, the general public, do not share?

One of Agnes's brothers died at one hundred and a sister at ninety-seven. Geneticists in labs around the world are examining the longevity genes from her family and others to try to figure which ones are "genes of long life" and how they are transferred but they may never unwind the complex structure of life, with all its variables. I believe that a number of the clues that scientists are seeking may have nothing to do with genes. If they listen closely to Agnes, they may hear some of the answers in the whimsical tunes she sings to herself.

1892

Anna DiFelice

Born March 10, 1892
Montepagano
Italy

E ACH TIME I have set off to photograph someone for this book, I have tried to
stay in the present, to observe and not to judge. My casual view of their current
surroundings rarely has given me any insight into the histories of these hidden supercentenarians. As I drove through the homogenized landscape of gas sta-
tions and chain stores in America, the predictable fast-food outlets and the
standardized care facilities never prepared me for the diversity and individuality of
the elders I encountered. Like delicate time capsules, they held reserves of cherished
memories of a world long past.

In central New Jersey, I found three generations of the DiFelice family gathered
together at a Catholic nursing home. The family had given me permission to visit the
week before and I rushed to photograph and interview Anna DiFelice. A frail woman,
walking slowly but deliberately, Anna entered a sitting room of the care facility on the
arm of her daughter. Using short sentences, she spoke to her daughter in Italian. Her
voice was soft, often trailing off to a whisper. Her story was difficult to piece together.
It was weeks later, actually, when I corresponded with her grandson, that I received a
more detailed picture of Anna's life. I find it inspiring that her grandson knew so
many details of his grandmother's life and showed such an intense respect for her.

Anna was born in Montepagano, a small, walled, medieval town that sits above the
sea in the Abruzzo region of Italy. Montepagano was fortified against the Turkish and
Viking pirates, and I am told it retains many of its original charm. Below the walls is
the much newer and better-known beach town of Roseto degli Abruzzi, where Anna
spent most of her early years growing up. In those days her parents had wheat fields,

and olive and mulberry groves that ran to the sea. The mulberry trees were cultivated for feeding silkworms, raw silk being one of three cash crops (along with wheat and olive oil) that were sent to the towns of Como, Lucca, and San Martino to produce the finished goods. Life as the town knew it changed during World War II when the war front went through the town. The German army camped in the olive groves and in the winter cut and burned down the branches for warmth. Much like the book *Corelli's Mandolin*, today part of Anna's family property is now a private German beach club. As a young girl, Anna would walk the beach and collect a now extinct mollusk as a breakfast food. Much like the ancient clam, her way of life of a century ago is all but extinct.

Like most children of the time Anna did chores, but the heavy work was done by hired help. In addition to general chores around the house, she helped to cook and tended the silkworms, which she found intriguing. She went to school for a few years and learned to read and write. As a young woman she saw a lantern slide show put on in the village. One of the pictures was of the majestic, newly built Brooklyn Bridge. She was so moved by the image that she vowed to see it. When she had enough money, she went by steamer to America to visit her uncle. Later, she traveled to Philadelphia to stay with relatives and remained there because she fell in love with a young man, newly arrived from Italy, who delivered bread to her uncle's house. He courted her and they were engaged within a short time. At the beginning of her married life they lived in a Belgian community in Philadelphia and, oddly, she learned French before she learned English. Her married life, however, was much like that of housewives in Montepagano, with her days filled with cooking, making sausage and wine, and preparing game, fish, and vegetables, all brought back by her husband from his many hunting and fishing trips.

Unlike many of the arranged matches of the day, Anna and her husband married for love. She has lived without him since 1958 when he passed away, seemingly a lifetime ago While for some it is a blessing to live to be a supercentenarian, for others the idea of outliving most of one's immediate family can be a curse. For those few of us who are touched by chance meetings with people like Anna, we are able to see history come alive, through an encounter that bridges our present with a past, bygone view of life. Speaking with Anna, I couldn't help but feel that I was in the presence of the matriarch of the family; the reverence she received was undeniable. I feel certain that Anna's family structure gave her a kind of social sustenance that has allowed her health to endure, and that nurtures her as she had nurtured them.

Catarina Carriero

Born January 9, 1891
Penha Garcia
Portugal

SOME PEOPLE HAVE BEEN EASY TO TRACE and photograph and others have presented a challenge. Years of production work in a photo studio taught me the patience required to locate many of these supercentenrians. Catarina took three months to locate, validate, and arrange to visit. I flew to Lisbon and waited to hear from my contact person who had been patiently translating and calling on my behalf to the village where she lived. When I arrived in Lisbon, however, I was told that Catarina was not feeling well and hadn't been out of bed for a few days. I waited each day at the hotel for a sign that she was well enough to be interviewed. For three days, I heard nothing and then, when I was beginning to lose hope, I received a call at ten one morning telling me that I could photograph her that afternoon. Unfortunately, the translator could not accompany me. It was a four-hour drive into the eastern part of Portugal, an arid, underdeveloped area very close to the Spanish border. My girlfriend and I had to rely upon our feeble vocabulary to communicate in a region still harboring resentment from the Spanish border wars.

Finally, we arrived at the village of Penha Garcia, which sat atop a small mountain. After navigating quiet, cobblestone streets with little shade and only a few road signs, we managed to ask for help from one of the only people we saw. The mention of Catarina's name, along with much arm waving and gesturing, led us to her house. Actually, the house belonged to Catarina's son, with whom she lived for a few months, alternating between his residence and her daughter's.

Catarina was born in Penha Garcia in 1891, one of six children. Her mother died when she was very young and her father lived to be 105. She had three sisters and three brothers, all of whom had predeceased her and none of whom had reached the age of ninety.

Her father was a stonemason and owned a windmill. From early childhood, Catarina used to help her father in the windmill. She took the family's donkey and went to get wheat and rye from farms nearby to be processed at their mill, and then returned with the flour. She never went to school and never learned how to read or write.

Catarina was married in 1914 to António Pascoal Nabais, nicknamed the *"Avô"*– hence Catarina is now called *"Ti Catrina d'Avó"* which means Aunt Catarina of the Avó.

Her husband was born in 1891 and died at the age of eighty-eight in February 1979. He was an agricultural laborer and owned two cows. She helped her husband with the field labor and was a dedicated housewife. She did not have time for leisure and was known for always taking care of everything. She worked with her husband on leased land near Spain, in Vale Freitoso. Catarina has never traveled far from Penha Garcia. She has not even been to Castelo Branco, the district capital, only a short distance away.

Once as a young woman Catarina was caught in Spain with a friend of hers while snatching fruit to feed their cattle. They were arrested and held for a week in Cilleros, Spain. Other than that, one of the highlights (the pun is intended) of her life was when she was struck by lightning. It missed her by a few inches but did strike her hat and left it in ashes.

At the age of 100 she was in very good health and spirits. Now, as she moves closer to 113, her eyesight and hearing are failing and people have to yell in her ear to be heard. Catarina believes her faith has kept her well. She has always been religious, but is now unable to attend mass, or to watch it on television as it gives her headaches. However, she still prays daily with her rosary with the help of her children.

Because the translator didn't come with us, the family found someone in the village that spoke French. So Catarina would answer in Portuguese, the neighbor would translate into French, and then my girlfriend Cheryl would translate the French into English. It was a little slow, sometimes comical, and at times tender. As Catarina spoke of the wars she had lived through, when there was barely a loaf of bread to share with all her children, her eyes filled with tears and she hugged my girlfriend's arm. As we prepared to leave, she cried again, kissed us, and stood in the doorway waving to us. We were both touched by the experience and sat silently with our thoughts as we drove back to our hotel. Though she was alone, a frail figure in her black shawl, I knew she wasn't lonely. Her life had been celebrated by her family, by her entire village, in fact. Now, years later, the images of that afternoon still return to me. Seeing Catarina made me feel a very personal responsibility to prize each elder. As Madeline L'Engle said in Mihaly Csikszentmihalyi's book *Creativity*, "Chronological isolation is awful and chronological segregation is one of the worst of the segregations." I agree, and I believe that if it takes a village to raise a child, it also takes a village to honor our elders.

Anna Peskey

1891

Born August 5, 1891
Cavour, South Dakota
U.S.A.

T HE STATE OF SOUTH DAKOTA is only two years older than Anna Peskey. She
was a young girl when President Benjamin Harrison appointed the last terri-
torial overseer to be the first governor of the new state. The year before her
birth more than 250 Lakota men, women, and children were massacred by the
Seventh Cavalry in what came to be known as the Wounded Knee Massacre. Anna was
born during an important era in American history, at the crossroads of the nation's
turbulent expansion and an inflection point in the twisted growth of our nation.

It took me a while to get to De Smet, South Dakota. After a few planes, lots of waiting time, then a long drive across land as flat as a tabletop, with countless vistas of
corn and soybeans extending to where the sky met the ends of the fields, I finally met
Anna Pesky.

Born Anna Kopplin in 1891 near Cavour, South Dakota, she has spent her entire
life living within a five-mile radius of her birthplace. Her mother died in childbirth,
leaving her at the age of eight to take care of her five siblings with her father. In winter, she attended a rural one-room school before there were differentiated class-
rooms and grades. Anna completed her sixth reader but abandoned school for good
to help at the farm. The other seasons demanded her labor and attention for the survival of the family and relegated her schooling to a low priority. Chores, preparing
meals for the family, even learning to bake bread were all part of her daily routine as
she became a teenager. Anna shouldered the work like a pioneer woman. On Friday
nights, there were neighborhood dances, but the rest of the time was about work. Her
earliest chore was herding the cows. "There weren't many fences back then," she
said. Anna learned to milk cows, took care of the chickens, and twisted sheaves of hay
for fuel when the farm ran short of wood.

In 1912, she married Oskar Peskey whom she met at the Iroquois church. They
moved to a farm near Cavour where Anna remained after the death of her husband in
1946, until the age of ninety-two. Her son Armand says she still asks about how the
crops are doing. He continues the family tradition of farming.

Anna has multiple generations of living descendants, including two living children, fourteen grandchildren, and over one hundred great-grandchildren. As her

daughter told the local paper, "We get to the great-great-grandchildren and then it gets a little mind-boggling."

If I could venture a guess, living a simple life was a component of this woman's longevity. She attended chapel every day. Perhaps her genes are the overriding factor, or the luck she had in surviving tornadoes and blizzards, but to listen to Anna and her family, it's her grit and determined perseverance that guided her throughout her life. Anna Peskey's ethic of hard work and clarity about her purpose in life may be a comment to us all that health and longevity are not as complicated as we think.

1892

Minnie Davidson

Born December 18, 1892
Bogator, Illinois
U.S.A.

MEMORY IS MADE UP of fragments of images, impressions, and recollections of events. As I started to write about Minnie Davidson, I couldn't get the image of the shoebox full of deckled-edged snapshots and scraps of old letters out of my mind.

"Here, I've brought some of my mother's things for you to see," Minnie's son Gordon said.

"So who's this?" I asked. It was a worn picture, like a daguerreotype from Mathew Brady's era, of a group standing in front of a stark, unadorned farmhouse.

"That's the family, that's the farm," the son said.

He handed me the shoebox of memorabilia and was very happy to sit next to me, going through item by item that illustrated parts of his mother's life. He seemed so devoted to her and I, new to interviewing at the time, felt some discomfort rummaging through a total stranger's life in a box. Minnie sat there in silence, looking straight ahead. She seemed to be struggling with something.

Minnie was born the seventh of eleven children in Bogator, Illinois. She went to a country school up to the eighth grade. She married in her early twenties and moved to a small farm in Jasper County, Iowa. Her remembrance of the trip was that they took three or four horses and a milk cow on a train to Laverne, Iowa, to their new farm. Long winters and a simple existence best describes her life. Life outside the farm was spent at the Methodist church a mile up the road. She had three children and lived on the farm until the age of ninety when she moved into the Good Samaritan Care facility. The absence of what we today would call creature comforts could define

her life in the Midwest. She seemed to have lived by stresses of nature and the rhythms of farm life.

Minnie didn't seem well. She wasn't conversant. She sat stoically to be photographed. There were parts of her life that her son couldn't recall or never really knew but, unfortunately, she didn't provide some of the answers that would have helped me to fill in the different periods of her life. She seemed distant, not quite engaged with the photo session. It was news, however, for the town. The town's newspaper reporter and photographer came to cover the event of Minnie being interviewed for a book.

As I was driving across the prairie, I received a call on my cell phone from the director of Minnie's care facility.

"Minnie passed away after you left. I thought you might want to know," he said.

It was my first loss on the project. Clearly it would not be the last, but I was unprepared and it saddened me. Unlike a doctor or someone on the frontlines of care, I was unaccustomed to death. It was a vague idea that you hear about or read about, but there was an unreality to it. I wondered if Minnie knew how near she was to the end, and whether she had perhaps held out for me to get there.

Mary Norris

Born February 29, 1892
Weepingwater, Nebraska
U.S.A.

T HE DAILY ROUTINE OF LIFE on the plains of America has changed little over the last few centuries. Sure, the landscape has been transformed by the inventions of electricity, the telephone, the automobile, the airplane, and now the Internet, but the rhythms of the Midwest remain pretty much unchanged, dictated by the vagaries of nature. This is a land of agriculture where the day begins before the sun rises and people go to bed just as it is getting dark. It is this kind of life, the simple life of the rural Midwest, that Mary Norris was born into at the end of the 1800s.

At the time of her birth, the Pawnees, numbering four thousand, made their home on the plains in the vicinity. The Lakota, their numbers dwindling as the West was divided, were settled on a reservation nearby. Mary was born into a family of twelve children in Weepingwater, Nebraska, the daughter of a molasses maker. She worked before school doing her chores and with a family that size it was like working in a commune, for the good of all. There were diversions. As a young woman she went up in an early-model biplane with a boyfriend at a local county fair. "It was a thrill," she said. "It cost a whole dollar!" She married young and moved seven miles away to another farm with her husband. Her life was hard by today's standards—up early milking the cows, separating the cream to make butter, walking behind a team of mules to plow the fields. Her physical life was almost indistinguishable from that of any other farmer's wife.

There was, however, an intellectual side to Mary. She had always been an avid reader, and from an early age she had a great love of learning. Somehow, in the brief pockets of time when she wasn't working, she managed to escape into her books and discover worlds beyond the fields of Nebraska. She became a teacher in the town's one-room school. She had thirty-five pupils ranging from the first to the eighth grades. She began teaching Sunday school in her thirties and taught until she was ninety-six. Her husband died when she was a young woman, leaving her to take care of the farm, which she did until the age of 102.

When I asked about Mary's early years, I was told that life involved adapting to harsh conditions. Mary's family was very poor but there was always enough food to eat. She was grateful for what she had. Later in life, living by herself, she never felt

alone or unhappy. Her faith was very important to her. She had reading and gardening and animals to fill her time. She felt that that she was being looked after.

Throughout Mary's long life, she had taken in stride the century of inventions and
"newfangled" conveniences that changed the country. What gave her inner peace was
her belief system, her profound sense of a force that was larger than herself. She
seemed to derive her strength from this core of faith that had been unshakeable
throughout her life. It had helped her through the deaths of loved ones and the rigors
of farm life. I know she was infused with the same sense of deep faith that gave comfort to so many of the supercentenarians I had met.

Catherine Kral

Born November 15, 1891
Holstein, Nebraska
U.S.A.

HYPNOTIC ROWS OF CROPS flashed by me as I sped down a stretch of road in Nebraska. It reminded me of movies I had seen about the prairie. As I drove along, not another car in sight on the hot August day, listening to opera on the radio, I could see a huge grain elevator at the edge of my view. I sensed I must have been getting near the town of Campbell, Nebraska, I was looking for. The fields parted and a small, neat town of about four hundred people appeared and then disappeared as I drove right through before I knew it. I found the nursing home where Catherine lived and asked if there might be a hotel or motel in town. The closest one was nearly thirty-five miles away so I headed out to look for a meal and a place to stay for the night. The road, perfect and straight, bisected farms and prairie, with an occasional herd of cows or horses in the distance. Somewhere along the way, I unknowingly passed the farm where Catherine had been born in Holstein, Nebraska.

The next morning I met part of the Kral clan at the nursing home. Paul Kral, the sole surviving son, was a farmer and still talked to his mother about the crops and the weather. He knew a good deal about his mother and he appeared to be extremely attentive to her. She sat straight-backed and alert, and while her hearing was not perfect, she seemed amused and concentrated on my every movement as I set up my equipment.

The farming in the area developed as a result of the Homestead Act of 1863, which allowed anyone to file for a quarter-section (160 acres) of free land. While towns took a while to be established, the population in the open lands grew rapidly and the need to communicate between farms increased. As a young woman, Catherine would go to someone's home for Sunday church where a traveling minister would preside. For socials, and dancing, she would have to travel by horseback two days to Hastings.

I asked about the dust bowl of the 1930s and the Depression to see if the country's trauma had affected her. "There was enough food to put on the table but there was never anything extra," she said. It may be that the hard life of farming had prepared her for the hardships of the Depression. It was hard to imagine this person in front of me, her posture erect and her eyes clear, having seen and experienced one of our nation's greatest ordeals, especially when you looked out on all the bounty of the surrounding fields. A reserved woman, her silence could have signaled her reticence to reveal her private life, or it could have been just a reflection of the sound of the prairie that surrounded us. While I had been given the privilege to meet Catherine, I nonetheless felt a twinge of disappointment knowing that, like all supercentenarians, there were parts of her history that were irretrievable.

Dora Mattingly

Born January 21, 1892
Washington, Kentucky
U.S.A.

ALL OF THE INFORMATION about Dora Mattingly came from her grandson who had been the recipient of stories that had been passed down by family members. Dora could not or would not speak. Her eyes, when she looked at me, were clear and sharp. She gave me the impression that her history, the history of the rural South, rich, almost cinematic, lay locked inside her, never to come out.

"Dora, can I ask you a little bit about your life?"

I was alone with Dora in a large, empty cafeteria. A kitchen staff person walked through and asked us to excuse her. As we sat there in the middle of the room, I quickly realized that I was intruding too. I was spending too little time with a person who didn't know me, a morning with a stranger, an outsider, to expect personal details to be instantly shared.

Born Dora Simpson in Washington County, Kentucky, on a modest farm, Dora grew up during an era in which in this part of rural America little had changed from the century before. She and her husband, George Washington Mattingly, lived far enough out of town that they would travel by horse and buggy to get two weeks' worth of salt, flour, sugar, and other essential supplies they couldn't grow or barter. They wasted nothing in those days. Dora's grandson was told that his grandmother would make the children's shirts from the flour sacks. Tobacco was the cash crop of the farm, but Dora and her husband also cultivated corn and hay for the animals.

Dora bore her children in the farmhouse, attended only by the local midwife. According to the family stories, she was never sick and never needed to see a doctor. The family chronicles included a few colorful details such as that her nephew used to wear two six-guns in town; that Dora would sit on her porch drinking shots of whiskey and quilting; and that Dora started dipping snuff at the age of ten and still does occasionally when she can get some. She worked her whole life in a distillery and managed to rear three grandchildren when her daughter died.

Dora underscored a feeling that was beginning to develop in me as I went from place to place in this country. There is a dignity that is inherent in the supercentenarians, protecting them even at their advanced ages. But there are many forgotten elderly people around them, remembered on certain holidays but otherwise living every day between those dates, waiting, marking time.

Emma Verona Calhoun Johnston

Born August 6, 1890
Indianola, Iowa
U.S.A.

WHEN I MET Emma Verona, I thought there had been a mistake. I figured that Robert Young in Atlanta, a man who manages the data for supercentenarians around the world, must have verified the wrong person. Emma greeted me in her bedroom, looking up from her crossword puzzle, exchanged pleasantries in a clear, spry voice, and then walked, without assistance, into the other room. A small woman of perhaps five feet, Emma looked eighty, with sharp, alert eyes and a strong handshake. What I was witnessing was one of the phenomena of supercentenarians, that they rarely look their age. They have the ability to grow old more slowly than others, the "Shangri-la effect," as I call it. I was told that in good weather Emma would walk to town to go to the beauty parlor. I had a remarkable morning with her.

Emma was born in Iowa, the eighth of nine children. Her father, who served three years in the Union army during the Civil War, became a Presbyterian minister. Emma mentioned that he found the war memories so horrific that he didn't want to talk about it. In her childhood days, Emma's mother and father would hitch up the horses and go away for the day to visit parishioners. It was left to Emma's older sister, Lulu, to care for her and mentor her. Her father had to balance his religious calling with raising food for eleven people. The family had to raise chickens, butcher hogs, and can food from their orchards to sustain themselves. It wasn't an easy life. They had to maintain a producing garden, scrub clothes on washboards, make their own soap, and periodically fill their mattresses with straw. They had to pump water from the cistern daily. Emma remembers that the family was very closely knit, that togetherness began with breakfast and then Bible reading in the living room before school. She and all her siblings went to college after being taught at home and at the town's church school.

Emma feels that the automobile was the greatest change of the last century. "It took our country from an agricultural to business society. I was in high school when I had my first automobile ride. A Stanley Steamer!"

She was asked whether times were better one hundred years ago. "Some things are so much better today. We didn't have luxuries then as we do now. Today we are cleaner, houses are cleaner, and the food is more varied and safer . . . but I think it's hard to judge 'better.'"

"But would you go back?"

"I wouldn't go back for anything," she replied.

Emma highlighted many of the qualities of the supercentenarians that I had seen from my travels. She considered her greatest accomplishment the bringing up of her children. When asked about her longevity she replied, "Be careful about choosing your parents. Make sure they have good genes." Her devotion to her faith and her daily reading kept her sharp and alert. Her diet, her sense of humor, and her ability to cope with life has made growing old a graceful process. "I still enjoy life, I still enjoy living."

Linus Reinhart

Born July 28, 1892
Kirby, Ohio
U.S.A.

D URING WORLD WAR II, Linus had three sons missing in action. The family was amazed that he accepted this with a kind of inner tranquility. All came back. One had been a prisoner of war for twenty months, another a survivor on a ship that went down, killing seven hundred men, and the third was saved after his ship sank at Iwo Jima. " He just took life as it comes," said Linus's son. When I met Linus, though his sight and hearing were impaired, he seemed still to be taking life as it came.

The Reinhart family used gold from the California gold rush to buy four hundred acres of land in Kirby, Ohio. When Linus was born, the family still lived in a log house that had been constructed by the local Native Americans. He could remember the natives' wooden huts without windows in the fields behind their house. The family farmed the land to produce their food and they hunted and gathered together as well. Linus recalled that, as a young boy, the family once went out to pick mushrooms for dinner, and mistakenly picked poisoned toadstools. Only because the children were picky eaters did they manage not to get sick. After eating the mushrooms, Linus's father and the local minister died. At thirteen, Linus was given the responsibility of running of the farm with his eight siblings and his mother. He milked cows and grew crops. When World War I began, he tried to enlist but since his three other brothers were already in the service, the recruiting officer told him to "go back to the farm; we need food more than we need men."

During the Depression there was enough food to eat on the farm, but, since live produce such as hogs was selling for so little, it was more economical to sell the grain.

Linus developed a variety of seed corn that sprouted consistently and matured faster than native corn. His pioneering of the corn germinated into a seed company, L. A. Reinhart & Son Certified Seed. He became one of the pioneers of hybrid corn in the United States.

An extremely religious man, Linus never raised his voice to his children, and although strict, preferred to discipline his children by taking them aside to "talk some sense," one on one. His son said that he was never "derailed by an obstacle. He just sat down and figured out how to get around them." These are simple enough concepts but Linus applied them to everyday life, abiding by his set of golden rules. He was an honest man, a man who believed in his faith, and who worked for what he needed. His son said that perhaps his greatest gift to his family "was his example and the life he lived that made him a special person." In our current day and age, when the media bombards us with politicians, celebrities, and other role models that are fleeting and uninspiring, how poignant and refreshing it is to come into contact with the Linus Reinharts of this country, who remind us of what it means to be a light for others to follow.

1889

Swami Bua

Born 1889
Pollachi, India

I WAS VERY SKEPTICAL of a supercentenarian living in New York City. It was even more improbable to find a supercentenarian Indian yogi. But I did find one on the west side of Manhattan in a small one-bedroom apartment. A woman in Miami who had studied under him for years had given his name to me, and she said that he was in residence at a temple in Hawaii during the year. With a little bit of sleuthing, I found him, not on the other side of the earth but in my own backyard.

I arrived at his door, rang the buzzer, and waited a few minutes while he slowly unlatched the various locks. Greeting me was a compact man in an orange toga. He was barefoot, and his bare shoulders, flowing white hair and beard gave him a divine-like aura. His eyes had a sparkle and in the middle of his forehead was a paint-mark that I guessed was a caste mark, or a holy dot. He asked me to take off my shoes then shuffled back to his discussion with a woman who sat cross-legged in the corner of the living room. The room was empty of furniture; along the walls were photographs of the swami when he was younger, doing amazing feats of physical contortions and yoga positions that were hard to imagine a body being able to do. There was one image of him balanced prone on top of a wooden post, the fulcrum being his stomach.

I began to set up my equipment while the woman finished her hushed conversation with him. As she prepared to leave, she told me that she had flown in for the afternoon to speak with him. She was a student, a disciple of the swami.

Swami Bua, the youngest of eighteen children, was born with severe physical disabilities. His legs and feet were crippled and contorted and he apparently went into some kind of coma at the age of two. Assuming that he was dead, his parents placed him on a funeral pyre to be cremated. The heat woke him up and the family, thinking

he had risen from the dead, shunned him. The die was cast. He was sent away to lead a life as an outsider, wandering from village to village, seeking food and shelter from others. He spoke Tamil, his native tongue, as well as five or six other dialects. He learned to speak English under British rule. As a Brahmin, a member of the Hindu priestly sect, he lived as a vegetarian within a strict caste system to which he had to adhere. The people of India were colonial servants, producing goods and services for England. Swami settled in a village of three hundred, most of whom lived in thatched huts with just a few permanent roofs. He lived on fruit, vegetables, and a little rice. There was no such thing as extras or indulgences for the villagers. Families worked to feed themselves and keep thatch over their heads.

I asked the swami why he thought he had reached the age of 110. He replied, first, that in his culture one never spoke of one's age. "It is never uttered, it is bad taste." Second, "It is because of all God's grace, supplemented with good thoughts, good eating, pure vegetarianism, humility, no anger or jealousy, and loveableness." How could you not fall in love with a man who lived by these thoughts? I had this vision of Swami Bua, sitting cross-legged, surrounded by a circle of small children who would hang on to every word as he would tell a story; but it was only my idealized fantasy; Swami Bua was actually living life as an isolated old man behind a padlocked door. Yet he seemed genuinely at peace with his life.

As he sat cross-legged on a mat in front of me, he spoke of his life as his religion and his work of faith as his life. Then, in handwriting clear enough for me to read, he suddenly began to write a kind of benediction. "Blessed, blissful immortal Jerry, my sincere prayers for your divine grace, while appreciating your humanitarianism, more particularly to young children . . . God bless you Jerry, live long until the call comes."

He took out a large shell, almost like a conch, with a silver tip, that he held in both his hands. As I started to pack up my equipment, he began to blow a single note. Years of yogic practice had taught him to hold a note like Sinatra or Dizzy Gillespie, in part to relax himself and in part to exercise. As I left, he was still holding that note, his cheeks puffed out without a trace of audible breath to interrupt the powerful sound of the single tone of his shell.

He lives in his world, in a sort of state of joy, while outside Manhattan honks, careens, and argues its way through the day. It such a shame that he's invisible to the city. Genetics aside, the swami has found many of the simple secrets of longevity in his everyday life and lives by them every moment that he breathes.

Julia Doughtery

Born August 20, 1893
Lima
Peru

"I'm a ripple in the tide, I just keep going on and on ..."

I FOUND Julia Doughtery to be a slight but strong-looking woman with a tan that glowed from her summers in Cape Cod. She sat in a wing-backed chair with her hands clasped in her lap, lending her an air of tranquility. She lived with her two sons in a New England cottage not far from the sea. Her son Frederick Ekstrom took care of both his mother and his brother, who had childhood multiple sclerosis and was confined to a wheelchair. Each family member performed as caregivers to one another. This compassion for each other hung in the air and gave even me a feeling of comfort.

Julia's father was Federico Christian Bergman. He had been the vice consul from Peru to the United States and stood next to President McKinley when he was shot. Federico had represented the business interests of South America at the 1905 Expo.

In 1900, when Julia was a young girl, she and her family settled in New York City. They moved often, to Brooklyn, Washington Heights, Manhattan, Pelham, and Montclair, New Jersey, as the father's work dictated.

Life for Julia was gay during her teens and twenties. She attended many diplomatic parties. As a young woman, she sold war bonds during World War I and was personally acknowledged by J. P. Morgan. She was most effective in selling bonds because of her fluency in Spanish and English. She remembers going out to New Jersey and riding with "the handsome cavalry officers." Her cousin was married to a Colonel Nichols who ran the military base. Julia loved taking pictures on the week-ends. She would often travel with her father to Buffalo and Philadelphia for business. Life in the diplomatic service seemed carefree. In the end, she married a dashing young man, Gustav Ekstrom of Sweden. Even while living in the fast lane, she never smoked or drank, and was always conscious of eating well. Julia seemed to have dealt with the stresses of life events with calm.

The most significant thing to have happened to her in her life, as she was quick to tell me, was the birth of her children, not the telephone or any other invention of the twentieth century. Julia's first child was born with multiple sclerosis and spent many years at Johns Hopkins for treatment. When she was pregnant with her third child, her husband died of a self-inflicted gunshot wound while hunting. She never admitted it to her children until the daughter found out through the police when she was arranging for a passport. Julia managed to overcome her profound sense of grief and loneliness over losing her husband by joining an amateur opera company and singing in their productions. She was one of three sisters and was very close to the oldest. When her sister died in 1971, Julia took over the rearing of her sister's seven children.

She has been swimming most of her life and swam daily in the ocean up to the age of one hundred. She liked taking walks around her garden in good weather. Her mind was keen and she only regretted that she could not be more independent in her hundreds.

Julia had never been sick in her life until the age of 107 when she developed an intestinal disorder. Recovering swiftly, she settled back into a quiet life in her ivy-covered cottage bathed by the salted sea air. It was her little quote about being a ripple on the water that resonated with me. The poetry of the phrase, the simple understanding of her life, made me think that she had resolved her connection with the patterns of life and her sense of endurance. Serene, composed, like a ripple she understood the rhythm of life.

1890

Aurelia Marotta

Born June 27, 1890
East Boston, Massachusetts
U.S.A.

I N THE LATE 1880S, there were twelve families that lived on a small island off Boston Harbor. Aurelia Marotta's family was one of them, with no electricity, no telephones. The only means of transportation to the mainland, Boston, was by steam ferry powered by coal. As hard as it is for me to imagine this scene, it was even harder for me to comprehend the number of changes that occurred in Aurelia's lifetime

There was very little information that I could get from her or her son, an adoring man who came every day to feed her and spend time with her. She seemed agitated by my presence so after I set up my equipment, I waited patiently for her to finish her lunch and digest her food. I began to photograph her and probably had four or five images in the camera when she became aware of my being in the room and began to murmur, "Help." Her son tried to calm her but she increased her volume and eventually started shrieking, "Help!" at the top of her lungs. I quickly packed up my stuff and headed for the door. Her son was very embarrassed, but he shouldn't have been; I had disturbed her world and she didn't like it. Her son met me in the hall and we talked for a few minutes about her life.

He told me that when Aurelia was a young girl the family would ride with a team of horses to the wharf for the ferry ride to Boston. There were gas lamps on the streets and coal in the furnaces for heat. Schooners and tall ships still worked the shores of Massachusetts. She went to East Boston schools and became a secretary, but her life changed with marriage and a family. Her son said that his busy mother always thought that one of the greatest inventions to come along in her lifetime was the washing

machine. She had never been fond of a wash day that consisted of boiling a huge caul-
dron of water on the stove and cooking the clothes. Aurelia used to tell her son that
the family would hang a sign in the window with either "25" or "30" or "35" on it,
which referred to how many pounds of ice were to be brought upstairs by the iceman.
The rest of the details of her life were not known by her son and, unfortunately, were
now locked inside her.

I came away from this experience with a sense of frustration and sadness. Neither
her family nor I could not retrieve a lifetime's worth of experiences from this woman.
It was a shame. Her history could have taught her son and his children and deepened
their understanding of the family's past. She was part of an exciting story. There was
a richness of the maritime life of early Boston that I know I would have loved to hear
about; these stories transfer experiences and feelings among a family that both
enrich the next generation and validate a life by the telling of the tales.

1889

Joan Moll Riudavets

Born December 15, 1889
Es Migjorn Gran, Minorca
Spain

A<small>LL OF THE PEOPLE</small> I have photographed for this book have taken some time and often days of travel to locate. I had been corresponding for many months with Juan Pretus, a professor of evolutionary biology at the University of Barcelona in Spain. He was born on the same island of Minorca as the supercentenarian Joan Riudavets and knew his family. He had made the introductions necessary for me to photograph Joan.

I flew from New York City to Barcelona, waited to make sure Joan was well, took a small plane to the island, rented a car, and with a map found the tiny town of Es Migjorn Gran in the center of Minorca.

Simple, unadorned stone houses lined both sides of the winding, narrow, cobblestoned streets. The village was filled with a quiet that only comes from being surrounded by fields and pastures; Es Migjorn made sense as a place to nurture someone 114 years old. Birds occasionally broke the silence as they rode the wind from the ocean, swooped through the village, and then returned to the fields.

Joan grew up as one of ten children from two different mothers. His mother died days after his birth and it was not until he was an adult that he found out that the woman who reared him was not his biological mother. A few of his brothers and sisters died as children. At the time of my visit, Joan had two brothers over one hundred and two other siblings over ninety.

The values of the family have been carried from generation to generation. Joan's paternal grandfather and his father started the first company in the town, a successful shoemaking export business. Joan continued the family business with his

siblings. Joan's father earned his living at the factory to get ahead but, starting with the next generation, the family focused on education. They all read newspapers but Joan was the only one to go to school. Like his father, Joan was passionately and politically involved with the well-being of the town and he later became its mayor. Even though he was not monetarily rich, as mayor he was respected for his depth of righteousness; he was hardworking, peaceful, and devoted himself to spending most of his life, even out of public office, working for the benefit of others. This was consistent with his philosophy of life: to be respectful, to support freedom, and tolerance, and to adhere to a steadfast work ethic. During the Spanish Civil War he was removed from office by succeeding dictatorships and watched a bitterness grow in the village as his townspeople went hungry.

As I sat listening to Joan in a little cozy room off an interior courtyard, it was hard to imagine how tumultuous and filled with tragedy his life had been. He suffered the death of his wife, the death of his eldest daughter, and the hatred brought on by the Spanish Civil War. However, Joan was careful not to lose sight of all the extraordinary positive events of his life. He could look back and point to the day electricity was brought to the village, the first motorcar, and the changes on earth in his lifetime.

Joan's mind was still sharp, his humor still intact. He had lived by rules of conduct that had helped to predict how his life would evolve. As a moderate, he had sought solutions without conflict. He was very aware of proper diet and had eaten well, exercised, and worked hard; every night he was able to go to bed with a clear conscience. What is most extraordinary is that, at his age, he still puts himself to bed and gets himself up for the day. To Joan, life "is worth living because we constantly see that new things are discovered."

1892

Consuelo Moreno

Born Jan 31, 1892
Tangier
Morocco

The happiest moment in her life was "when I came to the United States." How few of us recognize what we have; we take so much for granted. Born of Spanish parents in the city of Tangier, Abuela Consuelo grew up in Morocco under a protectorate agreement between France, Spain, Germany, and the United States at the end of the nineteenth century. Tangier was thus an international city at the time, and Consuelo grew up during one of Tangier's golden eras. She was educated through elementary school and, after her father's death by drowning, she was apprenticed to her mother to become a seamstress. At the age of twenty-four, she married and with her husband, opened a restaurant. They ate what they served and as they had plenty of fresh produce and olive oil in their diet, Consuelo developed life-long eating habits that a nutritionist would envy. "So what do you think has helped you to reach such an advanced age?" I asked.

"Eating little, never worrying about how much we ate, lots of olive oil and garlic," she said. In between helping out in the restaurant's kitchen, she managed to have nine children. She was a devout Catholic who believed in God. She never smoked, she drank very little, she never learned to ride a bike and she never learned to drive a car—she walked to most places she had to go.

During World War I, she was on a Senegalese ship bound for Casablanca when the cannons of a German warship began to fire. They had to sail without lights through the night in order not to be noticed; it took six turbulent days to reach Casablanca. Consuelo had been afraid but felt God was watching over her.

While I was photographing her, I asked, through her daughter who translated, what were her recollections of Tangier were. She became teary-eyed, as the image in the book reflects, and repeated a few times, "My Tangier, oh my Tangier" lamenting the changes that she has seen in her lifetime. Her thoughts turned to happier memories: being a child running to the beach late in the day; playing with her friends by the ocean as night fell. It was a simple time, a wonderful time that still lived within her. I would have stayed longer but she was off to lunch and I was holding her up. I recognized that the history of Tangier in the twentieth century was held inside this woman. Perhaps she had communicated to her children or grandchildren what she had seen or felt, perhaps not. I only hope her family knew to ask. As I was leaving, one of the last anecdotes came from her daughter who told me, very proudly, that her mother was the oldest naturalized citizen in the history of the United States. Consuelo Moreno became a citizen at the age of 106.

1893

Maebelle Plant

Born February 26, 1893
Brantley, Alabama
U.S.A.

I ARRIVED IN NORTHERN FLORIDA after a long drive from Alabama. I found the house of Maebelle's daughter Caroline on a quiet back street off a main thoroughfare near their church. I met Maebelle in her rocker in the living room. A delicate woman with a gentle smile, she extended her hand in greeting, a hand that felt like a feather in mine. Her eyes twinkled with clarity. Her gaze was one of inner peace and perhaps a little amusement that I had come all this way to hear her stories. What I discovered as we spoke was that this placid, smiling woman was a living history lesson.

Two of Maebelle's maternal great-great-grandfathers served in the Continental Army as the colonies fought for independence from England. One served as a partisan soldier for General Francis Marion and the other for General George Washington at Valley Forge. One of her grandfathers served in the Civil War as a captain in the Florida militia.

Maebelle was born in a one-room log house with a stick-and-dirt fireplace. Her first responsibility as a young child was to make sure the fire was out before everyone went to bed. The beds were trundles to conserve space and the "outhouse" was an area behind the smokehouse. Water was taken from a dug well, shoes in those days were in short supply, and food was cooked on a wood-burning stove.

The family sharecropped from morning to nightfall just to survive. In the dark of night, lit only by a candle, her parents would gather the children before bed and they would have Bible reading and prayer. Sundays were always set aside for rest and giving thanks. The family walked to church a half-mile away; Wednesday and Saturday nights they would have prayer meetings where participants would share their problems. This early childhood rigor, with an appreciation for what little they had, gave Maebelle her tools for life and portended her future.

Maebelle married at nineteen and she and her husband became sharecroppers. A few years later she had a "religious experience" that changed her life. The words of God spoke through her, told her to follow the church's path, and from that moment on she served her religion. "I had this intense desire to be filled with the Holy Ghost. My sister, Myrtle Franklin, came to the house and began to pray for me. I was gloriously baptized and began to speak with other tongues as the Spirit of God gave utterances."

The Depression was hard on her family, and Maebelle and her husband, Lee, lost their life savings. Together with their eight children, they moved into a small farmhouse "on someone else's place." Maebelle considered it merely a bump in her life's road; she coped and moved on. She and her husband were focused on building the Pace Assembly of God that was the start of her missionary work and teaching which would extend throughout her life.

Of the supercentenarians I have photographed, Maebelle was clearly one of those whose life was defined by her faith. Her daily hard work, her beliefs, her disdain for "idleness" seemed to have been part of her secret not only to longevity but also to a better quality of life. As she sat rocking in her chair, a smile of contentment crossed her face and her keen eyes inspected me. Had I understood what her life had been about, her eyes seemed to ask? It seemed as though she had achieved something that few of us ever find—peace of mind.

1893

Lena Dionne

Born June 14, 1893
Lynn, Massachusetts
U.S.A.

L ENA DIONNE, THE DAUGHTER OF A BLACKSMITH, was born in Lynn, Massachusetts, a coastal town north of Boston, when commercial sailing ships still plied the waters off the Northeast. The year was 1893, during the second of Grover Cleveland's presidential terms. It was also the same year that Lizzie Borden was acquitted of the murder of her mother and father in one of the more sensational trials of that century. I stopped to think; that was two centuries ago. When I met Lena in St. Petersburg, Florida, she came into the greeting the room of her care facility, elegantly dressed, walking without assistance, wondering why I had come to take her picture. She seemed much younger than her years, perhaps in her eighties. I kept assuring her that she was important to my work and that her life story was worth telling. Her air of humility was refreshing. "Why would you bother with an old lady like me?" she said. "I'm very busy, reading trashy novels and loving them."

"So what was it like to grow up in your family?" I asked.

"We had a wonderful time. My parents worked in a factory and my grandparents raised us kids." "And were they strict?" "Why, we were sent to our room without food if we misbehaved," Lena quipped. "But we had a fun life. Sometimes when I put my head down at night I think about the wonderful things. I loved to roller-skate . . . that's what I remember the best."

She had been employed in a shoe factory when she was a young woman. Lena married at sixteen, and she and her husband lived "up north" before moving to Florida in the sixties. Her husband died shortly after moving south, and she lived by herself up to the age of 106.

The photo shoot was conducted with Pastor Judy, Lena's best friend, who took great pleasure in being her spiritual guide, sitting just outside of the camera frame and talking to Lena. Lena could recall events without any prompting. She was also demonstrative, not shy. Lena told me after ten minutes that I had taken enough pictures and the session was over. Pastor Judy and Lena prayed together as I was wrapping up my equipment after the session. Although Lena's immediate family was no longer alive, she had found a surrogate family in the nursing home director and in her minister. On Sundays, she would walk to church, connecting one house, where she was cherished, to another house, that she cherished.

She was an extremely devout worshipper who lived with a certain acceptance of the inevitability of life. She read the Holy Scriptures as well as her Harlequin romance novels daily, both with devotion, I might add, and without the need of glasses. Reading seemed to be one of the keys to keeping Lena so energetic and alert. Her connection with her faith seemed to be another key that grounded her.

If you trace history through the three centuries that Lena has lived, some of the great events of modern times have punctuated her life. At ten, she learned that the Wright Brothers had flown a plane at Kitty Hawk, North Carolina. And at the time of the presidential elections of 1920, she rushed to the polls to vote. She hasn't missed a single opportunity since then. She has seen all the wars and all the inventions. Her parting wisdom, when I asked what advice she would give to help a child live so long a life, was, " Eat a good breakfast, it starts the day off right."

Hendrikje van Andel-Schipper

Born June 29, 1890
Smilde
Netherlands

MY ONLY REGRET was that I was unable to go on to higher education," said Hendrikje during the course of my meeting with her. Girls of the 1890s generally didn't go past the sixth grade so, Hendrikje, the daughter of the headmaster of a local school, returned to her house to learn domestic skills while her brothers continued their studies. Clearly a bright woman who laughed and joked with my interpreter and me the day she was photographed, she was also amazing in her ability to remember details from her youth. I'm not sure I have quite such a memory.

She was given one of the first bicycles in Holland, imported at the time from the United States. My Dutch friend, who acted as translator and navigator in Holland, laughed when Hendrikje recalled the cost, 180 Dutch guilders, which was an enormous sum of money in those days. "I was active all my life," she said. She rode her bike until the age of ninety-nine when she broke her hip and had to move into a nursing facility. While I marveled at her age, it was her vitality that was so inspiring. It seemed as though she assumed everyone could or should be as equally vibrant, feisty, and inquisitive. Actually, why was I so surprised?

She wanted to let me know that she thought she had lived so long because she had been drinking Geneva, a Dutch gin, since the age of ten. While there is no scientific proof that gin is the elixir of life, Hendrikje said with conviction that she thought it had been in her case. She examined my face for a reaction. I think she was enjoying the experience of meeting someone new, being a bit provocative, seeing what response she might initiate. Energetic and full of life since youth, it was a bone break that slowed her down and changed her life. She has outlived her family and most of her friends. Living in her neat, small apartment surrounded by curios and her pictures, I was reminded that people like Hendrikje outlive everything but their memories.

1892

Sara van Grondelle-Bloom

Born December 6, 1892
Purmerend
Netherlands

SARA VAN GRONDELLE-BLOOM looked up at me with a big smile as I entered the room. Her two sons, ages seventy-four and seventy-nine, stood up to greet me. One son lived in Alberta, Canada, and was in the Netherlands for his yearly visit. The other son lived in the area and each day took his mother to church, morning and evening, for her prayers. As the brothers explained her life to me, I understood that I was with a woman whose faith and religion has guided every aspect of her life.

She spent her young adult life as a housekeeper in a doctor's home and there met a young man, Maring van Grondelle. It was love at first sight. They went boating in their spare time but worked very hard and were God-fearing people. They were members of the Dutch Reformed Church, where Sara sang in the choir. They married in 1918 and had six children. She led a quite life but for an ocean liner trip in 1957 to visit her 102-year-old sister, Mien, in Canada. The sisters were both devoted to Bible study all of their lives, singing and living by the Scriptures of the Old Testament and the teachings of Calvin. Unfortunately, the two sisters drifted apart and no longer speak to each other. Sara confided that Mien does not recognize the new interpretation of the New Testament and feels that Sara has become impious and "lost her way."

It seems that this unswerving faith has been the backbone of Sara van Grondelle's health and happiness. While she may not be as ultrareligious as her sister, she was plainly devout. While I was watching her, Sara broke into religious song, with a voice as clear and filled with vigor as that of anyone half her age, and her sons joined in. It was one of those special moments, when something as simple as a song sung by someone aged 110 made me stop, take a breath, and celebrate.

1892

Lucy Victoria d'Abreu

Born May 24, 1892
Dharwar
India

H OW OFTEN IS ONE cordially invited to a party by the Queen of England and the Duke of Edinburgh? At 110 years of age, Lucy Victoria d'Abreau was asked to visit with England's monarchs, who recognized her as Britain's oldest subject. Although it interrupted her daily nap, she found it enjoyable, but a bit tiring. A little sacrifice for the royal family broke up the day. Lucy has witnessed quite a lot in her time: she has lived through the reigns of four other monarchs, experienced three centuries, seen the invention of most modern technologies, and traveled halfway around the world to settle in Sterling, Scotland.

Born in the town of Dharwar in southern India on May 24, 1892, she was named by her ardently pro-British parents after the reigning Queen Victoria. Raised by her moderately well-to-do family in a Christian community, Lucy was educated at a local convent school. Her brother was the first Indian bishop of Mangalore. She addressed the servants in the household in Hindustani but she would otherwise converse with family and friends in English. Her memories of her childhood in India are filled with days of badminton and lounging under the casuarina trees. She "stayed at home and looked around until somebody came and claimed my hand." That someone was a "dashing" young doctor to the Queen Mother, named Abundius Joseph d'Abreu, who later become a cousin to the royal family by marriage. Lucy and Adundius were married in 1913 in Mangalore.

During World War I, her husband served in the army in Palestine and was befriended by an Irish colleague who suggested that when the war was over he could assist the doctor in establishing a general practice in Waterford, Ireland. After

successfully completing his studies in Edinburgh, d'Abreu qualified to become a surgeon and established his own surgical practice in Waterford. As soon as he could he sent for Lucy to join him. Together with their three children, Lucy booked tickets on an ocean liner and sailed for weeks to the docks of London and then by ferry ride to Ireland. The year was 1925.

The family prospered and grew with the birth of two more girls and a son. Tragically, their boy died of meningitis at four. The couple became Irish citizens and, with Lucy by his side, the doctor's practice flourished and he introduced the first X-ray machine to southern Ireland. He tended the sick and wounded during the Irish civil war and because they were Indian and were considered neutral, the family was spared the suffering of a country torn apart by strife.

Life was genteel and comfortable. Open house days and musical nights filled their lives with social events. Lucy and her husband became the founders of the Waterford Bridge Club. Like so many who lived through those times, World War II rearranged their lives. The war forced them to dig up their tennis court to plant vegetables and they cut peat for fuel at their home, which was named Grianbhrugh (Mansion of the Sun) in Gaelic. When her husband died in 1971, Lucy remained in Waterford and lived independently until she was 93. She then moved to Sterling to be near a daughter after a debilitating fall at the age of 106.

Still an avid reader of books, Lucy continues to keep up with current events through the daily newspapers. Her memory is keen; she could still recite Sir Walter Scott's epic poem "The Lady of the Lake" and, given her age, didn't show the slightest bit of confusion. Content and happy, her only disappointment seemed to be her diminished hearing. She reminded people that she's "as deaf as a post." Her daughter, however, had no trouble communicating with her while I was shooting her portrait. Lucy continues to impress all who know her with her daily walks, although she now uses a walking stick to steady herself.

When it was time for lunch, she was given her daily small sherry in the drawing room and I packed up to leave. The road out of Sterling took me into the moors and the mists of Scotland. During hours of driving through a vast empty space with little to interrupt my thoughts, I remembered that Lucy had said she had no secret to her long life. Perhaps she was right—there was no "secret" to her longevity. After all, she was frank in her declaration that she took "everything in moderation." No secret, but a lesson that served Britain's oldest subject well.

1893

Kathleen Gregson

Born June 13, 1893
Loughton
England

T HERE ARE TIMES when it is hard to understand the past, and it is often harder
to draw inferences from it. For me, the end of the Victorian era in England,
even with reference to historical records, is difficult and sketchy at best to
imagine. It was another culture, another time. Driving up to a baronial manor
perched on a sandy bluff overlooking the Irish Sea set the stage for a new compre-
hension of history. I was welcomed at the door by nurses in starched white uniforms
who ushered me into an elegant living room and offered tea in bone china cups. I was
first introduced to Miss Gregson's grandniece and shortly thereafter, I met Miss
Gregson, who was brought into the room in a wheelchair. The moment she spoke,
with her clear Thatcheresque delivery, she escorted me back in time.

The 1890s were an age when social differences began to dissolve, when the opu-
lence and gracious living of the Victorian era gave way to the momentum of techno-
logical and social change of the Edwardian time. The "Gilded Age" formed the
backdrop for Kathleen to grow up in England during the beginning of international
conflicts and before the horrors of World War I. Miss Gregson's articulate recollections in her refined educated accent painted a reality of her life that was reinforced
by pictures from her family album. She was born in Loughton, Essex, on the edge of
Epping Forest. Her grandfather built their home on his land and called it Hearts Hill.
The house included a farm where the family kept a herd of Jersey cows. Kathleen's
earliest memory as a toddler was that of her nanny in the nursery hanging her "nap-
pies" to dry. As a young girl, she would stand at the garden gate with the family's two
Irish wolfhounds to say good-bye to her father in the mornings. Miss Gregson was

educated at home by her governess until she was fifteen. She remembered the names of the cook and the maid, Emily and Minnie, "who had left their situation to move to our home in the country." Often my questions would bring answers tinged with dry humor. I asked her if she recalled her childhood fondly. "Goodness, yes, I didn't give two hoots about anything. It was carefree. I don't think my parents had any worries either."

The horse-drawn carriage and an age of innocence gave way to the automobile and the industrial revolution. Kathleen was one of the first women drivers in Britain, and frequently would navigate the length and breadth of England and Wales on her travels visiting friends and relatives. "The First World War changed England, changed everything," she said. Though she had been studying at the Royal Academy of Music, she soon left to help her country. "I must do war work," she decided, so she volunteered to cook and be a driver at a Red Cross hospital in London. Unlike other women of her class who preferred the safety of their parlors, Kathleen witnessed the savage devastation of soldiers who had lost limbs or were fatally wounded. She recalled "the dreadful wounds" of the young men who had served on the front lines and the "the horrible gas" that racked their bodies. She was at their side, a reminder of the gentility they had left behind, giving them comfort in the midst of war's chaos.

After World War I, Kathleen moved back to the country where she taught school in a local village. During World War II, the German air force attacked their neighborhood and a bomb exploded down the chimney. It destroyed the house but, miraculously, she and her mother survived. In fact, she wasn't conscripted because she alone was taking care of her mother. She moved a few times but ultimately bought a small house with a garden where she remained for thirty years among many friends. She has a great love of animals and nature and even into her nineties was a very keen gardener. She told me that early one morning she fell down the stairs. She paused and I respectfully asked she if she broke anything. "The teapot," she said, with all the timing of a polished comedian. She was then ninety-nine years old. I asked her if she was getting tired from the interview and she replied, "No, actually I'm fine. Talking about my sticky past. I'm rather amused." I asked why she thought she might be as old as she is, if there was some insight that she might share? "I think the Devil's got hold of me and he won't let me go," she said as I broke into laughter. She sat in this grand room, motionless with a wry smile on her face, a measured cadence to her speech, gentility in the tone of her voice. "Either the Devil or God's got hold of me."

1893

Doris Prater

Born October 26, 1893
London
England

FROM HER MAJESTY'S FAMILY upstairs to the people in service downstairs, the British Isles have shown me such contrasts of life that it's often given me pause to think. I drove into Rugby at twilight, which in England in early December seems to begin at three in the afternoon, through a steady drizzle and fog, and finally found a small, kempt house on a quiet lane, my destination after an all-day drive from Liverpool.

All smiles, Doris Prater seemed to appreciate the company and all the fuss of lights and cameras as she sat in a rocker in the living room. She had been living with her daughter and son-in-law for many years, and they appeared to be a tightly knit, warm and comfortable family.

Doris was born in London. She attended school until the age of fourteen. She was a plucky child. Near the end of one school year, she leaned over to talk with a friend in class and failed to hear the question that the teacher had asked. When she was called upon to answer the question, she couldn't respond. The teacher took her from her seat and caned her. When the headmaster asked her about the caning, she replied that it was her first and her last, that she was leaving school. He asked what she was going to do, if she had any prospects, to which she replied that she hadn't. He offered her a job as a nanny in his home, taking care of his children, and so began Doris's life in service. This job lasted until she enrolled in a cooking school in Demster Hall. She began with the traditional teachings of cleanliness: scrubbing floors and pots and pans. Her dream was to become a pastry chef but she was called back home to take care of her ailing mother. There she remained, taking a job in a factory making lamp filaments for BTH national utility. She married but lost her husband when he was thirty-eight. The rest of her life was spent "downstairs" in service to others.

Doris was one of the most cheerful of all the supercentenarians I photographed. There was joy in her face that seemed to come from her closeness with her daughter and a gratitude for her surroundings. The lesson of Doris Prater supports one of the silent secrets of the supercentenarians, that longevity is enhanced by a sense of family, or in some cases, community, which provides the warmth and security of belonging.

Kame Higa

Born June 22, 1892
Okinawa
Japan

KAME WAS THE FIRST PERSON that I photographed in Japan, and though somewhat jetlagged, I was nonetheless excited by the prospect of meeting supercentenarians from a country noted for its reverence of the aged. On a hill above winding, narrow streets in Okinawa, my translator and I found a clean, quiet home for the aged. Kame's doctor, educated at Stanford University, who spoke perfect English and could not have been more cordial, greeted us at the door. Kame herself was somewhat reserved, wearing a yellow woolen hat she had knitted and accompanied by her only daughter, eighty-three, who lived at the same care facility.

Recurring silences punctuated the interview. The translation process cut into the flow of the dialogue and produced an awkward cadence that made all of us a little uncomfortable. I also sensed that I was missing some of the nuances of Kame's stories and only hearing the facts.

Kame was born in Naha-city in Okinawa, not far from where we were. When she was born, the city had one train line that took people from the harbor. There weren't even real roads, only grooves in the dirt for the wheels of the horse carts. She could remember helping her parents with chores on their farm. When she was in her early twenties she married a Japanese sake peddler. He would fill bottles with sake in Shuri (near Haebaru-city, Okinawa) and carry them to Katena-Yanabaru (to the north) Together they had seven children. While the yearly years of Kame's life were hard, the later years were even harder. She worked as a housekeeper and at the same time managed the family's small farm to support her family. There were pigs and goats and she grew beans. Kame made tofu and miso soup, but mainly the family subsisted on tofu. She worked from early morning to late in the night. She and her husband led this simple, struggling life until war came. When World War II broke out, the government conscripted him and he died in the war. Their first and third sons also died in combat.

During the conflict, Kame fled from Okinawa and didn't return for four years. When she returned to the island she found that there was nothing left—no homes, no farms, little to sustain herself and her family. She and her children lived in camps without floors and they slept on the ground. It took ten years to achieve a better

standard of living. At the age of sixty, Kame and her daughter began life again, open-
ing a variety store selling incense sticks, matches, ice, and candies. She worked most
days until the age of ninety. She had sidestepped death, illness, and the hardships life
presented; it's as if her inner gyroscope kept her balanced while adapting to each
change.

Kame was never seriously sick or had medical issues until the age of one hundred
(when she slipped and broke her hip). When she did get a cold she would boil *funa* (a
kind of fish) and drink the broth. Her religious training was not formal but she was a
strong believer in respecting her ancestors. As a believer in Shinto, Kame held a
basic optimism about human nature and a natural feeling of worship that connected
her to past generations. Her relationship with her daughter had a different context,
given her Shinto beliefs, than I could understand as a Westerner. Her close bond with
her daughter made me think of my childhood, when you were asked to "pair up with
a buddy" in order to go swimming. Kame seemed to have embraced a lifelong buddy
system with her daughter which, like exercise, eating, or faith, provided a nurturing,
supporting environment to help her endure, often in the roughest of deep water. Her
motto was "Always respect older people and ancestors." It seems even now she
believes in the same motto and respects her elders, though there are few who are
older now.

1894

Mitsu Fukushima

Born August 8, 1894
Okinowa
Japan

FOR EVERY RULE, there are exceptions. I would have thought that Mitsu Fukushima would have been an unlikely candidate to live to the age of 110, but the fact that she did underscored the point that genetics can override many other factors, and it can help a person endure, even in the absence of a nurturing environment. To me, sadness is a killer, or at least it contributes to illness: Mitsu had more than enough sadness to go around.

Mitsu was born in a rural village of three hundred houses. The father grew potatoes, and rice, and all five children worked to sustain the family. Mitsu managed to get to the third grade in school but dropped out to help in the fields and around the house. The government collected a certain amount from the crops and whatever remained was left for the family to live on, which for them was very little. Mitsu remained at home until she was twenty-three, when she met and married a man who lived in the next village.

When she was pregnant Mitsu's husband, who was a policeman, found work in the Kanto area of Tokyo. He had a strong sense of responsibility and was on duty the day of the great Kanto earthquake in 1923. He sacrificed his life to save others and never lived to see his child born. Two months later, his son was born to a grieving widow. Because of her fierce love for her husband Mitsu refused to remarry, although she received many proposals. Life became very difficult for her as a single mother. She sold matches on the street to support herself and her son and there were times when there was only enough food for Mitsu's son to eat. Through the years, her only joy was the loving relationship she had with her son, who eventually became a guardsman at

the U.S. army base in Okinawa. At the age of seventy-four she moved from Amami Oshima to Okinawa as she was getting old, the climate was better, and she could be closer to her son. Together they would go to the sea or to the mountains to commune with nature. This gave her serenity. Up to the age of 103 she would remark, "My age is one hundred and three, but I feel like sixty or seventy." When her son died, the light went out of her life. She preferred to be by herself, to be left to her loneliness.

The care facility attendant, a young man in his early twenties, said that Mitsu spoke every day of her wish to die. But she couldn't. Her heart was strong, and although she was weak because she didn't want to eat, she was nonetheless healthy. Here one could see the strength of her genetics at work. Her immune system was alert; her organs denied her wish to die.

As Mitsu lay in bed, turned away from me in her desire to be left alone, I was struck by a question that continues to resonate in my head. What is the balance between quality and quantity of life? Mitsu's life story, invisible to all but a few people, was a gift to me. She has influenced my thinking. Like peering into the universe, the extremes like time and distance often raise more questions than they ever answer.

Kamato Hongo

Born September 16, 1887
Kagoshima
Japan

ARRIVING IN KAGOSHIMA-CITY, across the bay from Mt. Sakurajima, one of the world's more famous active volcanoes, I looked forward to meeting the oldest validated person on earth. On a quiet street with a small banner hanging near her door announcing Kamato's stature as the oldest person in the world, I found four generations of the family gathered around her in a small living room on the first floor. Kamato sat in her chair, smiling. When I was introduced to her as "the person who'd come from America to take her picture," she grabbed my hand and squeezed it with glee in acknowledgment.

She was born on a small island of Tokunoshima in the Kagoshima prefecture. She was one of five children, the second daughter of a fisherman and rice farmer. As she described it, there was nothing in the village—no electricity, no cars, no streets, only dirt ruts for horses and carts pulled by bulls that carried rice and sugar cane from the fields. The focus of daily life was on providing food and shelter for the family. This left little time for anything else. Kamato never went to school and her days were spent playing with her siblings and helping out around the house. She was an honest and easy-going child and admitted that she was spoiled when she was little. At seven, she experienced the first of many wars, the Russian-Japanese war of 1894. At seventeen, she lived through the second Russian war with Japan in 1904. She recalled that as a teenager she and her sister would stroll through the town in their best kimonos and were "conspicuous because of their beauty." At twenty-one she was introduced, in the traditional Japanese way of the time, by her older brother to a man from the village whom she married. He was a farmer and together they raised sweet potatoes, peanuts, sugar cane, and seven children. Her first was born when she was twenty-two.

The hard times of her life occurred during the years of World War II. Kamato remembered the air raids from the B29s and the times the family spent hidden underground. She also recalled the shock of receiving a letter conscripting her first son into the army. He survived the war and died at the age of eighty-six. Her first daughter died at ninety-two. Kamato had her *butsudan*, her family altar, in the corner of the house. She used to pray every day for her family, giving rice and changing flowers out of respect for her ancestors.

If attitude is a component to longevity, Kamato's belief in not worrying has kept her healthy. She used to say, "Don't steal others stuff" and "Do the right thing" to her children and she seems to have lived by these simple rules. Because she never had the chance to go to school herself, she always urged her family to "study, study, study." Her support of them was returned; they have showered her with love and affection.

From her same village was born a man, Shigechio Izumi, who died in 1986 and reportedly lived to be 123 years of age. Studies of longevity have indicated that the water on the island is unusually alkaline, being filtered through coral. Others have studied the medicinal value of the green tea of the region. Kamato, along with her national celebrity status, had packages of green tea with her picture on the bag.

If she has a formula for her long life and health, she believes it to be hard work and eating raw sugar from cane every day. While I photographed her, she sang and laughed with everyone. I was offered the brown cane sugar. Yet what I was most struck by was how much her whole family adored her. I watched as her seven-year-old great-granddaughter came in after school, dropped her backpack of books, and immediately hugged Kamato. This little girl in her blue school uniform does this every day; her little ritual, just to say hello. No one can know the formula for longevity, but this little girl may be a basic ingredient that kept Komato smiling, spirited, and young for her years.

1891

Sawayo Tanaka

Born June 9, 1891
Matsuyama, Shikoku
Japan

S AWAYO WAS ALERT and waiting for me when I arrived at the Yukuhashi Memorial Hospital. I could see by her hands that she had worked hard during her life, and she shook my hand with a power you feel more often from a person of sixty or seventy.

Her father had cleared fallow land in the 1870s and put it under cultivation. He planted fruit fields and his business prospered. When Sawayo reached nineteen or twenty, her father looked for a suitor who could partner with the family and continue to grow the farming business. He found a young man in the next village suitable for his daughter and arranged that they should marry. She had little say in the match.

Sawayo and her husband moved into her parents' house in Yukuhashi after their marriage. They planted pears, grapes, and figs and the fields enlarged over the years into a prosperous farm. Sawayo had five sons and three daughters. She had always been a spiritual person but became extremely religious after her second daughter was born. As a follower of Tenrikyo, a relatively new religious sect of Shintoism, she often went to the mountains to a shrine to pray. During World War II her first son died in air combat. From that day until she moved to the hospital in her late nineties, her routine was to walk twenty minutes or so every day to pay her respects at her son's tomb.

Sawayo has two daughters, eighty-nine and eighty-eight, and a third daughter who is in her mid-seventies. Her fourth son is alive and almost eighty years old. She spoke about her country life, her diet of fruit and spinach, and how her lifestyle contributed to her longevity. So, too, her deep faith kept her from succumbing to the

grief she endured during the war. It would appear to my amateur eyes that Sawayo's coping skills built a stable path for her to live a long and healthy life. At this end of her timeline, Sawayo seems to have avoided most illnesses. Her personal habits have allowed her to arrive at a place of happiness, surrounded by a community of her family. I am convinced that beyond passing on her genetic code for longevity, she has passed to her children her code of behavior.

Mitoyo Kawate

Born May 15, 1889
Hiroshima
Japan

"There was a flash and an enormous sound."

ON A SUNNY DAY, my jetlag behind me, I went to visit a woman who had survived the atomic bomb at Hiroshima in 1945. I carried with me a lifetime's baggage as an American. What I found was a petite, delicate woman with a smile, sitting in bed. One of the first things I was told was of her wish to emigrate to the United States. I photographed her in her room but as my translator had some difficulty with a few details, and Mitoyo had some difficulty speaking, we interviewed one of her closest friends who also lived at the care facility.

Mitoyo was born in the Hiroshima prefecture. Her father had gone to America as a young man after Japan emerged from isolation. He dreamed of becoming rich but returned to Japan disillusioned yet happy to be home. By the age of sixteen, he had married, had four children, and became a farmer in a nearby village. Mitoyo did not go to school for economic reasons but learned to read and write on her own. She remembered playing at home—cat's cradle and homemade beanbags and spinning a top carved from an acorn. In the fall she would go to the mountains to gather chestnuts for the family. She took care of the cows and horses with her brothers. Her parents arranged a match for her and so at the age of sixteen she married her cousin and began a new life as the wife of a farmer.

She had four children, two of whom died before the age of seventeen. The family grew rice and had a few animals for their own needs. Life was simple and demanding, but they always had enough to eat. The government collected more and more rice to adjust to the demands of a country at war. It was 1945 and she was fifty-six years old.

Two elderly friends of Mitoyo, my young translator, and I sat in the hallway on a bench discussing the details of Mitoyo's life. The floors were shiny with wax and the sounds of the care facility were low with only an occasional murmur coming from the other rooms. Shortly after the women began to speak, my translator began to weep. The eyes of these elderly women began to well with tears, too, as they told the story of August 6, 1945.

"Food had been scarce and most lived on sweet potatoes and some rice," the woman said. "Our husbands had been conscripted by the army earlier in the year and had been taken away to a training facility in town, in Hiroshima. There was no news of them and no communication was allowed because of the war. August sixth was a warm, clear day and we were hanging the wash out to dry. There was a flash and an enormous sound."

I watched these women of different generations crying over tragic loss. I didn't need a translation for what I was seeing. The story told, of innocents who suffer the tragedies of their government, is a story of history, which repeats itself over and over on other sunny days.

After the war, life returned to the same rhythm of farming. Mitoyo farmed by herself or with the help of her children until the age of ninety-nine. She broke her fingers working and the bones didn't heal. Her children sold the farm and Mitoyo moved into the retirement home at age one hundred. Even at her advanced age, she volunteered to do work at the nursing home when she arrived.

Mitoyo was rarely sick during her life and never suffered from radiation poisoning or related illnesses of the atomic bomb. A thin, hard-working woman of stoic determination, she survived her history with a smile. There were life lessons in that smile. Observing others through the camera has helped me to examine my own assumptions and my own biases, pressing at the limits of my own ignorance. I left this sweet woman not quite able to reconcile all that I had seen, felt, and heard. She seemed to be a piece of the past, the present, and the future. Even today, I'm still walking around with a part of that brief encounter as I go about my daily life and read about the news of today, about yet another war in a different place and other women who will endure and face their lives without their men.

1892

Yoki Yonehara

Born March 2, 1892
Kamou-cho Ohara-gun, Shimane
Japan

I LEARNED THE DETAILS of Yoki's life at a noodle shop in Shimane. A building that sprouted up in the midst of rice fields, the noodle shop was an old wooden structure with a few chairs; it was warm and intimate from years of conversations and the smells of cooking, sake, and farmers. I was taken there as a guest by a relative who had come to meet me at Yoki's hospital. At the hospital, which was clean, bright, and antiseptic, there was a quiet bustle of activity; lunch was being served as I arrived so I had little time to talk and learn about Yoki's life. The nurses were so well mannered and kind, and wholly attentive to her needs, and were gracious to me even though I was obviously a disruption to their routine. Slowly, I packed up my equipment after the shoot, watching as Yoki was accompanied in her wheelchair to lunch. I was struck by the sheer number of care providers relative to the resident population in this small rural hospital, especially in comparison with what I'd seen in my travels in the United States.

Yoki was born in Kamou-cho Ohara-gun Shimane prefecture in 1892. Her father was a farmer and, like many country girls of that time, Yoki attended school only through the fourth grade. In order to help support the family, she took a leave of absence from school and secured a babysitting job. She had loved math and reading and taught herself to read *kanji* (Chinese characters). Later, she finished elementary school and went into service as a domestic until she met her husband, a man many years older. She had five children by him; two died very young and the others lived into their eighties.

Yoki's husband died when she was sixty-nine years old. Up until then, she had spent her life cooking and keeping house. She never served prepackaged foods and believed in the process of choosing the right foods to cook. She moved in with her eldest son and daughter-in-law after her husband's death and took care of their

children. She delighted in teaching math and she became actively involved in her grandchildren's school events because she felt it benefited the children. She also developed a routine of walking miles on Sunday to visit her husband's grave and listen to sermons in the Nazarene church she attended.

All of Yoki's children are now gone. She vividly remembered them passing and it clearly still gives her great sorrow when she thinks of them. It is hard to survive all your offspring. Yet, I believe that while those feelings of loss do not go away, they are somewhat softened by supportive surroundings. Yoki has had the good fortune of being nurtured by this hospital staff and by her countries' compassionate culture. I was but a casual observer, not understanding the language spoken but keenly aware of how it felt; it was the language of respect and appreciation I could hear. She seemed very important to the staff, not because she was the oldest resident, but simply because she was a resident. I was very impressed. I left there thinking how much the end of life seems predetermined by the beginning. The care that you receive as an elder in Japan is the same as the care first lavished on a newborn infant. My travels around the world have only deepened my sense of the disparity between the cultural riches of various countries. One way to evaluate the depth of a culture, its wisdom and spiritual legacy, is see how it values it elders.

1891

Tadanosuke Hashimoto

Born April 27, 1891
Ono-cho, Sanda
Japan

O N A COLD, RAINY MORNING, I drove up to a small private hospital on the outskirts of Sanda, Japan. Modern and clean with wide halls and brightly colored walls, the hospital gave me a feeling of calm as I walked past groups of fastidiously uniformed nurses speaking in hushed voices. While I set up my equipment in a large lounge-dining area, I was watched with curiosity by a group of residents. Mr. Hashimoto's family arrived and, after traditional bows and the exchanging of calling cards, the staff of nurses brought him in to meet me. Dressed in a perfectly ironed kimono, he sat in his wheelchair with a contented smile as his family began to tell his life story to my translator.

Tadanosuke's father died when he was four. He and his mother moved back to her hometown to live with her brother's family. Tadanosuke's grandfather was the postmaster of the area and as patriarch of a distinguished old family line, he was both influential and wealthy. Life was very strict and ordered for Tadanosuke growing up. When he graduated from school at fifteen, his uncle asked him what kind of job he had in mind for the future. Tadanosuke answered, "I would like to be a photographer or a tailor because these are new businesses with prospects. There are not so many people doing these jobs now."

So, his uncle took him on a trip to Osaka prefecture where there were numerous job opportunities. Tadanosuke was most impressed by the new Western-style military jackets that he saw hanging in the windows. At that time, the kimono was the standard form of dress for both men and women. He began to wish he could make such modern clothing as the Western-style jackets he saw in Osaka, so he decided to become a tailor. He went from one tailor shop to another until someone hired him to be an apprentice. In those days the iron was heated by charcoal, so he first job was to prepare the iron for his boss. He worked long hours, apprenticed himself to other tailors, and by the age of nineteen he was well prepared for his career. He also married a girl from his hometown before he was twenty and settled in Sanda for his life's occupation. In addition to his tailoring, he and his wife, Hanae, worked gathering fruits from his in-laws' orchards, planned their future and began their own family. They had seven children; four of them are alive today and in their seventies and eighties.

With his wife's help, they built a tailoring business with a good reputation. Those were the days of foot-pedaled sewing machines and hand-sewn covered buttons. Tadanosuke did the sewing, designed patterns, and made elegant custom suits. One of his first clients was the president of a furniture company, who was pleased with his work. More well-heeled customers followed and the young tailor's reputation spread. Throughout the next eighty-six years, Tadanosuke worked as a master tailor, winning numerous awards for his work in Japan. His last job, at the age of 102, was also a custom suit for the mayor of Sanda.

When Tadanosuke was 107, his wife celebrated her hundredth birthday and the town honored them with a festive party. After his wife died three years later, he continued to care for himself until the age of 109, when he had a stroke that left him paralyzed on his right side.

Like many of his countrymen, Tadanosuke has lived a structured and disciplined life. With little time for travel other than the family's yearly outing to a hot spring, he led a focused and hard-working life well into his hundreds. Perhaps his disregard for his chronological age, or the recognition he received for his craftsmanship well into his eighties, nineties, and early hundreds, gave him a sense of personal relevancy. I can't quantify the importance of his genetic strengths but I feel, having been with this man, that his life had the flair and quiet elegance of a well-styled suit, and kept him healthy and happy.

1893

Toukichi Kusumoto

Born June 10, 1893
Hatsushima, Arida
Japan

"In their personal relationships they are mentally a mixture of toughness and softness, often emotional and romantic to the point of sentimentality in their fantasies; but in real life and in marriage, their loving is not so sentimental but tenaciously loyal." Characteristics of the sign of Cancer, referred to me by Toukichi's granddaughter.

BORN JULY 10, 1893, Toukichi was born under the astrological sign of Cancer, and the above description was apt for this quiet, subdued man. Early one Sunday morning, I took a train to a peaceful town in the Wakayama prefecture of Japan and was greeted by Toukichi's grandchildren at the railway station. I wheeled my equipment through empty streets and silent alleys to a perfectly manicured little house. Removing my shoes, I walked on traditional straw-woven mats, passing through a sliding door to meet a man in a formal kimono resting in bed. Described by his granddaughter as a sober and strong-willed, he was known throughout his life for his diligence and stubbornness.

Toukichi had two older brothers who died at the ages of ninety-four and ninety-five. A sister and younger brother died of childhood illnesses. Like many other supercentenrians I have met, he possessed amazing genes that have been sustained by other environmental factors. His simple yet arduous lifestyle, his stoic approach to adversity, his place within a nurturing family, all seemed to form a framework within which he has maintained his health and vitality into his senior years.

Toukichi's father had been a rice farmer. After graduating from high school at the age of seventeen, Toukichi took a job at a local bank. He would walk forty-five

minutes to work in his *geta*, or wooden clogs, and then change his shoes. He loved to walk in his *geta*. This became a lifelong habit that he continued until the age of one hundred. His first salary was five yen a week, which would translate to about eighty-five dollars per week today. His hours at the bank were long but he rarely spoke of his workday when he came home. He saved his money and slowly earned promotions. His few indulgences were a phonograph and records that his grandchildren brought out in a box filled with mementos from his life. I was amazed to see old 78 rpm records, the covers in pristine condition. The box contained bits and pieces of items that held great sentimental value for Toukichi, from old currency, lotto tickets, and matches to an abacus and antique storybooks. Each marked a point in time, a passage point in his life.

While celebrating his eighty-eighth birthday, Toukichi's father choked on a rice cake and died. This was not the only tragedy to shape Toukichi's life; his wife died very young of tuberculosis, leaving him to raise his six-year-old daughter. As a young man with a child, he chose to move to the village of his wife's parents to provide a better life for his daughter. He also chose not to remarry out of love for his lost wife.

During World War II, Allied aircraft came over and bombed his town, leaving large craters and burning down many of the homes. Fortunately, his house was not hit, but the electricity was cut. Lights were out for a long time and he was forced to live by candlelight. So began his habit of collecting and saving matches and candles in case of emergency. After the war, he would wake early to go to the fields, where he would tend his vegetable garden before going to the bank. It was his way of making sure his family did not go hungry.

His diligence and his force of character paid many dividends throughout his life. He was devoted to his family and his simple wants provided him financial stability. Once, he was able to loan a friend money and was given original shares of stock in a weaving company as collateral for his kindness. His friend was unable to return the loan so he was told to keep the shares. Today that weaving company is called Toyota Motor Company and, like one of Aesop's fables, Toukichi's kindness has been returned many times over.

1892

Toyo Endo

Born Feb 13, 1892
Gotemba
Japan

TRADITION IS A WORD that seems to be absent when one describes life in most modern Western societies. Even in Japan, a culture that can look back to its roots in 1300 BC, tradition is succumbing to a Western pace that leaves little room for convention. Toyo Endo seemed to be the bridge between what was and what is. In a perfect little house in the suburbs of Shizuoka-city, Toyo lived with her eighty-eight-year-old son and his family, surrounded by both the conveniences of modern life and a traditional Japanese rock garden outside her bedroom. Rejecting the introduction of Western fashion, dressed in a kimono and *geta*, traditional wooded clogs, she has steadfastly held on to a way of life that seemed to give her continuity and strength.

Born near Mt. Fuji and Hakone, Toyo grew up in a household of structure and tradition. She was an outstanding student. She was sent to school in Tokyo at a time when it was rare for a girl to go to school away from home. She attended a Japanese dressmaking college and boarded with a family. The daughter of the house would talk to a curious black machine that had a deep voice. This was the first time Toyo found out about the existence of the telephone. Most of the townspeople in her village of Gotemba did not have electricity in their homes. When she returned to teach in Gotemba, Toyo's father was one of the earliest to receive a phone.

While she was working at her first job at the elementary school, the young principal became charmed by her and asked Toyo to marry him. However, her father, being a famous person in Gotemba, scolded the headmaster for not making use of a proper go-between. Toyo's father softened over time when he realized how interesting and serious the principal was, and eventually gave his permission. Toyo was twenty-one at the time.

Together they went to teach in a small village, Inno, on the way up to Mt. Fuji. In this small, agricultural town with only kerosene lamps, the townspeople had no interest in education. Refusing to be deterred, the new teaching couple set about to innovate. They created a boys' and girls' school and a library. She taught the girls manners and needlework. In eight years, the village became famous for its school system. The minister of education gave them a special commendation. Today, those in their seventies still remember Toyo and her husband and the educational achievements of this couple.

Toyo had six children. All are alive, from her seventy-one-year-old daughter to her eldest, her eighty eight-year-old son. In the living room of her house I was given tea and shown memorabilia. Many of the photos in the family album were of Toyo as a young woman, when the world had just begun to pick up speed. Looking at my Polaroids and then looking at the sepia images in the album, there was a strong visual continuum between the past the present. I was given a peek at Japan at the turn of the twentieth century in the twenty-first century. Yet, in the flesh, Toyo displayed an even greater reverence for her ancestry and tranquility than one can capture in a photograph.

Different traits of supercentenarians appear more unambiguous in some than others, and Toyo's social network stood out. Drawing from her family and school life was a rich social wellness network that gave Toyo a sense of belonging; these intangibles sustained her and allowed her to age with grace.

1892

Haru Shimazu

Born July 7, 1892
Nirazaki
Japan

SOME OF THE PEOPLE I have photographed don't have histories one would marvel at, yet are special in some way, the way all people are special if you bother to really look at them or listen closely to what they have to say. On the face of it, Haru's story was not exceptional. She was born in Nirazaki near Yokahama, where her father was a teacher. She went to school through junior high and married when she was nineteen. She had six children who are all now in their seventies and eighties.

Her life was organized by work. She would rise at 5:00 a.m. to begin her day of cleaning and sewing. She made kimonos and yukatas until the age of one hundred. She led a quiet, unassuming, happy life filled with caring for her family and volunteering to teach sewing in her neighborhood. She had lived with her son from 78 until she was 106, when she broke her hip at her front door. But there was something about Haru's spirit that couldn't be explained by any simple recitation of the events of her life. In her eyes there was a vitality, a lively sense of wonder. Though she was 111, she had an almost childlike innocence that took pleasure in a smile and an embrace.

When I photographed Haru, she seemed so cheery and happy I was there. When I showed her a Polaroid from the session, she looked up at me and beamed. When I was preparing to go, she held out her hand. Not only was I surprised by her strength, but also by the electricity that flowed from her. She pulled me down to her and gave me a kiss; she held on to my hand as if she didn't want to let go. For a brief moment, I felt she was saying thank you. Her face was filled with gratitude for the time I had spent listening to her. I was taken aback- I was the one who felt grateful for the privilege of

this afternoon. For what I had given her, I had received so much more in return. I believe that every human interaction produces unforeseen ripples, what is known as "the law of unintended consequences." This day I had intended to photograph another supercentenarian, but left with something more than a picture. I carried with me—and still do—Haru's appreciation for being told that she mattered, and that her voice deserved to be heard.

1893

Damchaagiin Gendendarjaa

Born January 3, 1893
Omnogobiamag
Mongolia

S TEPPING OFF THE PLANE at 12:30 a.m. into minus 26-degree air might sound like the beginning of a novel about traveling to another planet, but when I stepped off the plane into the cold morning air of Mongolia, I did enter a different world. The faces of small children lining the entry hall of the airport were unfamiliar to me. Smiling, ruddy cheeked with bright-colored jackets and tunics, laughing and craning to see their relatives, these children immediately set the stage for a different experience.

In the morning I was escorted to the Temple of Gandan in Ulaanbataar, the capital of Tibetan Buddhism in the country. Established as the state religion by Khublai Khan in the thirteenth century, Buddhism is at the core of the culture. The temple is a series of buildings of earth and wood containing a library of fifty thousand ancient books, teaching and living facilities, and houses of prayer. I entered one building to see the 26-meter-high gold Buddha, melted down by the Communist reign of terror and later rebuilt by the monks. Dark and quiet, the crisp air held the muffled sounds of boots on the stone floor. The very scale of the Buddha overwhelmed me as I stood at its feet. Out again into the bright sunshine, I was lead through a crowd of traditionally dressed older people gathered at the entrance of another lower building. Pulling back a heavy blanket concealing the doorway, I crossed into the sights and sounds of an important religious ceremony. As I breathed in the smells of incense and candle wax, I saw a small window high up backlighting the breath of the elderly people who were standing shoulder to shoulder in the freezing temple. The rhythmic chanting of monks, sitting in rows facing each other, filled the air. I was struck with awe at all of this. At the far corner of one row of monks lay an elevated green pillow, in what seemed like a place of honor. I lost all track of time as my interpreter ushered me on to the scheduled photo session.

We drove up to a Soviet-built apartment complex, a decaying concrete structure with the architectural flair of a prison. On the second floor, a smiling woman in her seventies greeted us, holding my hand as she escorted me into a small room. Sitting quietly on a low bed was a man dressed in yellow and gold silk with his eyes closed. His skin was almost flawless, his posture relaxed yet upright, and his hands rested peacefully in his lap. The woman said something in his ear and he gazed at me. I was introduced to the Lama of Gandan, the spiritual leader of the temple and of Tibetan Buddhism in Mongolia, the man who normally sits on the green pillow.

His life in many ways parallels the recent history of Mongolian war, revolt, invasion, and constant struggle. Born in 1893 in Omnogobiamag, the oldest of six children, he was chosen by his father, an herbalist, to enter the monastery when he was five years old. Educated by the monks, his studies were rigorous, but he recalled growing up like the other boys, getting into mischief and enjoying play. He recollected his parents' visits with him at the monastery. Life changed dramatically as Mongolia became the first of many Asian countries to fall to Communism. As Marxist doctrine took hold, seventeen thousand monks were arrested, shot, or deported to Siberia to starve. The monasteries were looted and razed until a cultural heritage that had stood for centuries was destroyed. Damchaagin went into hiding, returning to traditional farming on the steppes, retaining his religion in secrecy. During these years he didn't forget what he had learned as a young monk, and when Buddhism was resurrected in Mongolia after Gorbachev announced the withdrawal of the last Soviet troops in 1987, he continued his studies at the Gandan monastery.

His daughter was very proud of her father's accomplishments. She took from the wall a framed piece of yellow embroidered silk with old Mongolian writing. This was his *gavjiin damjaa*, his doctorate of theology, a Ph.D. received at the age of 106. Only ten monks have ever reached his status in Mongolia and she pointed out that his lama robe was sewn with a special black border to indicate his distinction.

As I was photographing him, he closed his eyes and prayed; his right hand enveloping amber beads that he used while meditating. He opened his eyes and looked with great stillness at me. I asked if his family was known for longevity. His mother died at eighty and his father at ninety. His youngest sibling, a brother, had died recently at ninety-eight. The reason for their longevity, he believes, was due to their food regime. "I have a strict diet," he said. "I consume very little meat, however, a lot of dairy products, rice, and vegetables are a major part of my diet."

After an hour, the lama became tired and wanted to rest. His afternoon would be spent in prayer when he woke. I was taken to the next room to continue to talk with his family while he slept. I was offered a small silver bowl with warm yak milk and tea. In it was the same kind that I had been told the lamas carry under their robes. For sanitary reasons no one else is ever allowed to eat from your bowl. Also, tradition has it that after a meal, one turns over the bowl and rubs the rim on a stone. Doing this over one's lifetime grinds down the silver so that the bowl becomes smaller. Mongolians believe that as they grow older they should reduce the amount of food they eat. I was told that Damchaagiin had never been to a doctor in his life, that he had all his teeth, and his only ailment was some arthritis that was beginning in his lower back.

Earlier, the lama had been asked about longevity. He replied, "Its great to be alive when you are not dependent on anyone." He said no words could describe the joy he felt about the fact that he could still dress himself and move about without the aid of a walking stick. I discovered that this word "dependency" had many meanings. His joy came from this contradiction of physical and spiritual reliance. His monastery, his fellow monks, his immediate family were all interdependent, and his long, rich life seemed to underscore this paradox.

As I had after meeting many of the people I have photographed, I left with a gift. The lama's daughter gave me a blue silk scarf as a symbol of health. But the scarf wasn't the real gift. I left Mongolia thinking over and over about this man, his health, his longevity, and his spirit. What greater gift could I receive than awareness?

1889

Mary Christian

Born June 12, 1889
Taunton, Massachusetts
U.S.A.

TWINKIES? I thought after hearing that Mary Christian, at age 113, had a passion for them. Hmm, maybe they possess some special health benefit, or maybe Mary carried a longevity gene that warded off the evil effects of Hostess Twinkies and other modern processed foods.

Mary's family moved west from Massachusetts in 1900 looking for better prospects. The town of San Pablo was recommended by a friend as "a little town with a lot of work." Mary had many jobs through her life; the first was in a chocolate factory. The great 1906 earthquake destroyed the factory and put her out of a job. She then became the third telephone operator for the Pacific Telephone Company. After marrying in 1907, she and her husband moved to Bakersfield where they had two children, both of whom died relatively early.

Mary's life was not out of the ordinary. She worked long, hard hours to support her family. She threw her husband out of the house one night when "he was drunk and womanizing" and lived on her own for the rest of her life. She led a simple life, a religious life. She was compelled by circumstances to work until she was ninety, and from what I heard, she was a resilient and optimistic person.

When I visited her, she had already lost her eyesight at 112, and her hearing was rather poor. She was one of many that I photographed who made me think about the value or quality of life versus longevity. Medical science has expanded our aging possibilities, yet living longer does not always guarantee quality of life. We take so much

for granted in our youth when health is on our side. Without exception, every time I have come in contact with a supercentenarian such as Mary I have thought about their mortality and my own. As often as not, however, one is bound to reflect not just on the issue of mortality and the value of life but also on how one's life had been constructed according to a paradigm of not so secret rules. As a lesson, while we cannot control our genetic code, many of the successful supercentenarian lifestyle habits can be replicated by us; at issue is the conflict of choice between our lifestyles and our health.

Charlotte Benkner

Born November 16, 1889
Leipzig
Germany

"It's a wonderful world, and I'm so glad I'm still here."

THERE ARE MANY WHO HAVE MADE THE TRIP across the Atlantic, gazed for the first time at the statue of Liberty in New York harbor, and found a new home in America. Few, however, can recall that experience as a child in the late 1800s, when the streets were cobblestone and the carriages rumbled along the docks carrying passengers from the boats. Charlotte Benkner arrived from Germany at the age of seven with her eleven brothers and sisters and remembers vividly the gaslights of Fifteenth Street and the pushcarts of lower Manhattan.

Once, during her days in early New York, she was playing with a group of children on the street when "we saw this thing coming down the street, making noise, without a horse." "Get a horse," they yelled in delight. It was the first time Charlotte had seen a motorcar in her life. We take so much for granted today but the impact of the automobile, the sheer newness of it, is hard for us to grasp.

Another childhood memory that stayed with Charlotte was of watching the man making his way down the sidewalk at night with his ladder to light the gas lamps. When we changed from gas to electricity, we also illuminated ideas and education and made a whole generation of potential discoveries possible. As if marking the span of time, Charlotte said she has lived through candlelight to oil lamps to gaslight and now electric light.

After Charlotte got married, she became involved with the Camp Fire Girls organization because she couldn't have a family of her own and ardently wanted to be involved with children. This began a lifelong relationship with the Girl Scouts organization, and she was recently recognized as the oldest Camp Fire girl in America (and undoubtedly, the world). Many of her fondest memories are of helping the girls, either buying them shoes, as many had none, or taking them ice-skating for the first time. Doing for others was so much a part of her life. She was active, always on the go. When I met her, Charlotte was taking care of her younger sister, Tillie, who was about to turn one hundred and lived in the same apartment.

Charlotte has said that she doesn't miss anything from "the days gone by." When asked what single event changed her life the most, she immediately replied, "The washing machine. It emancipated women from the washboard and was the greatest invention for women." She has proudly voted in every election since given the right in 1919.

Frequently, I have heard something during a meeting with a supercentenarian that would make me stop, put down my camera, and listen. "Live each day, enjoy it, make the most of it, do all you can and then be happy and content," Charlotte said. I listened.

Recently, I called to find out how Charlotte was doing. Her niece told me that Charlotte's sister, Tillie, had not been well and had passed away. Not long after, I received a phone call.

" Mr. Friedman?"

"Yes," I answered, not immediately recognizing the voice.

" I wanted you to know that Aunt Charlotte passed away."

"I'm so sorry. Did she pass quietly?"

"Ever since Tilley died, she has had no reason to live. She called out for her in the night. With her family gone, she had no reason to hang on. She died of a broken heart, I guess you could say."

Gladys Swetland

Born April 14, 1892
Mills, Pennsylvania
U.S.A

O N THE PHONE, Gladys wanted to make sure I understood that she should be going home to her house in Mills, a little town of 150 people; that there was no reason she should be kept at the hospital.

The hospital was an ultramodern building tucked away in the Allegheny Mountains. When I left the motel on my way to meet Gladys, the fog was so thick you could barely see the trees that lined the road, but you could hear the whine of logging trucks as they downshifted somewhere out in the mountains. When I arrived, the fog was burning off and for the first time I could see the simple homes and the town that was just a pass-through to somewhere else. In contrast, the sprawling, urban brick facility that could have been a school, a government building, or a prison seemed out of place, tucked away in the mountains.

To look at her, Gladys could have been seventy-five. She moved around easily. She spoke as clearly and lucidly as most people. At the moment we met, she was concerned about the well-being of her cat, left behind when her lawyer hospitalized her "for her own protection." I couldn't quite figure out exactly why she should be there either.

Gladys was born in a house that her father had built for himself. "He cut the boards from his sawmill when he was twenty-five," she said proudly. Her earliest recollection was, "I used to play in the lumber piles and sawdust, that's were I spent my time. Sometimes the piles would be as high as a house." She, her sister, and two brothers lived there together until her siblings married and moved away. Gladys never married. She told me that her father spent his time in the mill and her mother spent hers in church. Gladys became a teacher and lived for a while in Michigan, New Jersey, and Pennsylvania but would always come back home. She started teaching when she was eighteen years old in a one-room schoolhouse. When she had earned

enough money she used it to go to college. The family purchased a car, the Overland, around 1903 that replaced their horse and buggy, a two-seat surrey.

As I asked her detailed questions she became more animated, seeming to enjoy the retelling of her life and thrilled that someone cared to listen to her. She was proud that she had been healthy all her life other than "a bout of typhoid fever that set me back a bit." "She had a great life. I was the youngest of the family and my father was the main man in the town," she said chuckling. "I had my fun. I had my grandparents just two miles down the road and I went back and forth, back and forth. I had the time of my life . . . and then I had my Sunday school. I loved to teach on Sundays."

I asked her about major world events and Gladys grew quiet. "Every child in my school had someone in the war [World War I], the Second World War, too. Armistice day, the news came, all the kids jumped up, I let them run out of the room . . . out in the streets, people cheered, whistles blew. Gosh it was wonderful."

When I had asked Gladys what her formula was for a good life, she replied, "Your parents. They set the example. My mother was forever doing good."

Shortly before it was time to leave, Gladys asked if I would get back that way any-time in the future. I wish I could have said yes. Instead I hedged. "Maybe, you never can tell." I felt a certain sadness leaving her, giving her that answer; I expect no one would come to visit her. Periodically, I think of her and wonder if she ever made it back to her house in Mills.

1893

Minnie Kearby

Born April 14,1893
Ireland, Indiana
U.S.A.

"A Concurrent resolution wishing Minnie Kearby

a Happy 110th Birthday

Whereas, Minnie Armstrong was born April 14,1893,

to Warren and Carrie Armstrong on their farm in Ireland, Indiana:

Whereas, Mrs. Kearby attributes her long life and good health

to her "strength in the Lord" and "good clean living"...

Be it resolved by the Senate of the General Assembly

of the State of Indiana..."

S O THE STATE OF INDIANA recognized Minnie on her birthday. I'm sure her granddaughter remembered her on that day, but I wonder how many others remembered. She did not need a ticker-tape parade down the main street of Petersburg, Indiana. But it would be nice for the outside world to hold her hand a little. She told me wonderful stories that punctuated her life and gave form to her history and I saw how happy it made her to share them with me.

I tried to imagine who I was going to see that morning as I sat in an empty parking lot of the nursing facility. I was trying to guess what kind of a face went with the name Minnie Kirby. It was a crisp autumn morning with blue skies, and I could feel the season beginning to change. A white panel truck pulled up next to me, backed up to the door next to the entrance, and a young woman went inside. Moments later I looked

up to see her maneuvering a collapsible gurney with a body bag draped in royal blue into the back of the vehicle. A flash ran through me. "Oh, I hope that's not Minnie." The scene would have passed unnoticed if I hadn't been there. I had just seen the metaphor for the morning, maybe the project. So often, the elderly seem to pass unnoticed. However, that morning my fears about Minnie were unwarranted.

Minnie lived most of her life on a farm "somewhere between Ireland and the poorhouse," she would say. She recalled with ease her childhood memories of the soldiers in their uniforms returning home at the end of the Spanish-American War, and the Treaty of Paris that ended the war in 1898. "That was a happy time when the war ended. Everybody dropped everything." She was very specific about her recollections of growing up: how she carried pails of milk in the morning, churned the butter for the family and drove the oxen, their transportation, to church. She could remember her wedding, the buggies and wagons rolling up to the church, the wedding dress she sewed for herself. One of her saddest memories was of her brother going through the front door on his way to fight in World War I. She could also vividly remember the Depression. Yet those hard times were not what Minnie wanted to dwell on; she skirted the discussion. "You had to do the best you could," she said. "Many went through agony."

For some it would be a burden to carry so many recollections with them, especially the painful ones. Minnie put everything in perspective. For many of the supercentenarians, the way they balance life, the adjustments they make, maintaining a positive attitude reveals a coping mechanism they share that we would all do well to learn from. Minnie, like many of the other supercentenarians, became another important piece of the project puzzle; she also gave me another context in which to view the elderly.

1890

Elizabeth Bolden

Born August 15, 1890
Sommerville, Tennessee
U.S.A.

"MAMA LIZA, she'd be the person the family would go to, even neighbors, to get her opinion on a subject. She would counsel," said her grandson John. Surrounded by seven grandchildren holding her hand, talking into her ear, straightening her pink hat, fussing with her crocheted blanket, Elizabeth Bolden sat at the epicenter of her family's universe, at age 113.

Elizabeth was born to African-American sharecropper parents twenty-eight years after Lincoln signed the Emancipation Proclamation into law. Her life was a tale of two worlds in Fayette County, Tennessee. "Plowing, growing, picking cotton and corn was our family's livelihood," said John. Elizabeth sat listening to John but her age had taken the energy from her voice. "The deal was that the white landowner would take two-thirds of the cotton, three-quarters of the corn, we'd get the rest. So when it was time to do the weighing, like if we had twelve bales to weigh, the owner would say, 'These are twelve bales but they're shy-bales, not weighing up more than four good bales. So you get one, that's what you get. That was the kind of mathematics that was used." There were no arguments, no one to appeal to; you could hear in the voices of the grandchildren the resignation that their reality was toned by unfairness.

Grandson John continued, "They had no ownership. No, nada. They lived on one big farm, all the family. They had to eat, so the landowner would dole out so much during the year. Then come the selling, he would siphon off what was owed." The family would grow corn, not for cash but as a staple for both their table and as a basic feed for their animals. Elizabeth grew up eating organic vegetables, mostly what they raised in the garden, before the days of chemical fertilizers.

I naively asked the gathering of family members whether the reconstruction of the races had begun when Elizabeth was a child. There was a pause, followed by a loud "No" in unison. I guess I hadn't been clear, for one grandson said, "Mama's older sister, she was a slave. You know, like [those belonging to] Thomas Jefferson. There was a lot of fishing and such, but no mixing together. Why, the whole Tennessee wasn't mixed," the granddaughter Queen Esther said with a chuckle.

Elizabeth sat through this quietly, taking in the conversation but still saying nothing. Except for the occasional response, she was content simply to take it all in. I asked what they as a family thought was the most significant event in Elizabeth's life. "Wouldn't it have been when the family moved to that log cabin in Shelby?" Ezell said. "[The cabin] was already one hundred years old when we'd moved in. I was just a little, bitty boy. It was three rooms; there was a fireplace in the center for heating the winter and cooking. The children lived on one side and the adults lived on the other. School was four miles away. We walked, rain or shine."

"Did you go every day?" I asked.

"No, during gathering season there was no school," James said.

"Three months, no school. We went up through the eighth grade," Queen Esther said.

"And the school, what was it like?" I said.

"It was two rooms, with a kitchen and an outhouse. We had secondhand books, the old books from the white kids; we had all their names in the books when they finished with them."

The Grandkids mused about Mama Liza's religion. She was a devout woman, but church-going was restricted to one Sunday a month. "House service, that was every day; prayer service and Bible reading before they went into the fields and after they came out of the fields," said John. The services were conducted by Elizabeth's father, and then in later years by her husband for about half an hour.

"Was she stern?" I asked.

The question prompted laughter from all the grandchildren.

"She was known as the pipe grandmother," Ezell said with a laugh. "She smoked a corncob pipe, she was real friendly, but everything was on a schedule. Lunch was twelve o'clock, supper promptly at six-thirty, that's the farm way . . . and then there was the Mogen David wine she had to have every morning, before she'd eat her breakfast."

"One of the things I admired her for most," Ezell said, "[was that] she told you what she had on her mind and then she was through with it. She didn't grumble or moan about things, she could deal with it and move on."

I left the family talking to each other. I thanked them all for being so warm and

open to me; I thanked Elizabeth, she seemed to nod. I watched them together. The whole family seemed to be so together and alive in the moment; at that moment, I felt envy and a tinge of embarrassment for being white.

Bettie Wilson

BETTIE WILSON sat in her small, humble living room surrounded by love. Her granddaughter, great-granddaughter, great-great-granddaughter, and great-grandson moved in and out of the room to check on her but this almost regal woman sitting in her wheelchair seemed focused only on me, the curious stranger. I was struck by the deep respect, even in their speech, that the family showed toward her. "Yes ma'am, this gentleman is from the North," said Della, her great-granddaughter.

"May I ask him questions?" Bettie asked quietly. " Yes ma'am, I'm sure you can."

As she told me her life experiences, I realized that Bettie Wilson was a national treasure living on a back road in New Albany, Mississippi, just a short distance from the home of William Faulkner. Her recollections of her childhood were still wonderfully clear: the wood cabin she lived in, the long days of labor for her sharecropping family, her fidelity to her faith, and the stories of her parents fashioned a picture of a woman of no malice, with balance and grace, born of parents who were slaves on the Rutherford plantation at the end of the Civil War. She was the youngest of nine children. "My daddy was bought from South Carolina and brought here and my mama was born on the plantation. They took their names from the plantation's owner."

Bettie's earliest recollection was as a girl of four or five. "They'd leave me by the side of the fields where they were out working." She didn't get much of a chance to go to school, but she stayed on the farm helping the family. Nonetheless, she learned to read and at 114 she's still a voracious reader. "Mama has read the Bible cover to cover twice," her granddaughter said. Curious about Bettie's early home life, I asked if she could remember talking with her parents, Phoebe and Solomon, or if they talked to the family at the dinner table. "Not there, not [Daddy]. By my mama's side, then he'd do most of his talk, private-like but not that private . . . couldn't always get his conversation out like he'd want . . . he'd do his biggest talk with Mama." It seemed that Bettie's mother gave the family its moral guidance, teaching the children "like the Ten Commandments, like that, she did it that way."

"So, did you kids get into any trouble?" I asked.

"No sir, we didn't. I do remember going home with my oldest sister, Gussy; we go home the nearest way, down this private road, by this watermelon patch. My sister said, 'I'm going to git me a watermelon.' I kept that secret."

"So," I said, "you mean you've kept this secret for almost one hundred and eight years?"

"Yup," she said with a smile. She laughed, we all laughed. "Well, it ain't been on my conscience, it was no crime then, it was no big deal."

Toward the end of the Civil War, the Union army had advanced deep into the South. The details of who offered a rifle to her father were unclear to Bettie, but the moral lesson was not. "This man gave my daddy a musket and told him to go fight. My daddy said he would not; he would not kill a man. He set his gun upside a tree and walked off. My daddy said the Bible said don't kill."

Bettie's life was spent by the side of her now deceased husband, a preacher and farmer, for more than seventy-two years. After a long, full life and marriage, she had three children, twelve grandchildren, forty-six great-grandchildren, ninety-five great-great-grandchildren, and forty great-great-great-grandchildren.

I asked her, having lived so long and having seen so much of life, what advice she would give to children today. "I'd tell 'em, get a good job, choose one they like, and stick to it, don't jump around."

I left Bettie and the family but, in many respects, they are still with me. I think of her often. I've called her a few times. One image in particular stands out. I remember standing in the doorway, watching Bettie as she sat. In her hands, she held a cane passed down to her from her grandmother. Probably fashioned in the late 1700s, the smooth walking stick with its polished handle had supported three generations of women and they, in turn, had supported generations of their families, passing down not only their memories but their wisdom as well.

1890

Susie Potts Gibson

Born October 31 1890
Corinth, Mississippi
U.S.A.

S HE WAS GENTEEL AT 115. She was elegant. She was dressed for her portrait
and excited to tell her life stories with the sultry sound of her Southern drawl.
The first thing she said to me was, "You ever seen someone this old? I'm the
oldest woman in the world." She said this with a self-mocking tone and a bit of disbelief. I've met many supercentenarians, but perhaps no one as demonstrative and
talkative as she was. "Getting old isn't much fun. Try not to get old," she warned me.

Susie was from a bygone era of the South, a figure of refined Mississippi society
where women rode horses and played bridge, and the pace of the day was as slow as
the summers were hot. She was proud of her life, happy to share her stories. "I've
seen the good times and the bad times," she confided. Her recall of events and facts
from one hundred years ago was astounding to me.

"My granddaddy nearly owned Corinth," she began. "He said we could ride all day
on horseback and never get off our property."

During the 1860s, he "took his family to Florence from Corinth, Mississippi,
during the Civil War, to get away from the war," but they returned to live on the land.
As a small child, Susie mused, "All we had to do was go out in the garden and pick up
the pitty balls, they were all over the ground, we could collect a cigar boxful if we
wanted." The pitty balls were musket shot. The family lived not far from Shiloh, site
of one of the bloodiest battles of the Civil War fought under General Ulysses S. Grant.
Over 100,000 troops assembled for the battle, more than 23,000 troops from the
North and South died, a number equal to the battle of Waterloo, and yet the war continued.

Susie said her town of Corinth was so small you knew everyone.

"And we kids were sittin around talking and we said we could say nothing about anyone in Corinth because everyone was kin." She recalled that the first car in town belonged to the doctor, and when she was sick as a child, he promised, "I'll take you ridin' if you take your medicine, but he never gave me that ride." Transportation at the time was horse and buggy. "My father used to have the best horses, he'd buy race-horses that would quit racing." After a while, the bicycle replaced her horse and she rode the rest of her life.

Whether Susie rode a horse, bicycled, or walked, her church was her destination and the focal point of her life. She is a devout believer in the word of the Bible and has been all her life. "I pray all the time," she said proudly. Even in grade school she participated in prayer meetings, She prays at night and feels her life has always been in the hands of her God.

In rapid-fire images of her life, Susie described how she graduated from school as the valedictorian of her class, went to a business finishing school before going into the working world as a secretary at a hardware store. During the Depression, Susie ran a boarding house, renting out rooms in her home for extra income. An independent person and an avid fisherwoman, she would often go down to the river for peace and enjoyment. "By daylight, I would go down and just step into my boat." I listened in disbelief to her descriptions. It was as if it happened yesterday.

When Susie was a young woman, the Nineteenth Amendment was passed and women received the right to vote. "Lordy, it was such a long time ago, but I remember Teddy Roosevelt, and McKinley. They shot him!"

The more I listened, the more I understood Susie's value in the continuum of our history. Her faith and her life experiences can make us grow, for those who have the opportunity to listen.

Moses Hardy

Born January 6, 1893
Aberdeen, Mississippi
U.S.A.

SEVENTY-NINE YEARS AFTER he had fought in combat and won the distinguished Victory Medal of Honor, Moses Hardy received his recognition.
Brigadier General George S. Walker honored him on his 106th birthday by saying, "There are not many people around who have the opportunity to wear these
medals today." Yet, few Americans know about Moses, or what he did to give us, and
Europe, our freedom. It took the United States government seventy-nine years, more
than the average lifespan of most people, to acknowledge his valor. Moses is the oldest living World War I veteran of the 805th Pioneer Infantry, a segregated unit, and
like so many of the supercentenarians, he has dodged the minefields of life.

Moses was born and raised on his father's 265-acre farm in Wren community, not
far from Aberdeen, Mississippi. As the family story is told, Moses's father, who
owned the land with a Native American Chickasaw tribesman, bought the land for a
dollar an acre when the tribesman moved west to Oklahoma. The family has been on
the land farming it ever since, building homes on the property to accommodate an
expanding family.

Moses has had a companion all his life. Faith has traveled with him. Conviction
gave him a context within which to live. He never drank, smoked, or even ate meat.
Maybe he's the oldest vegetarian in the world. He doesn't take aspirin and doesn't
like the idea of doctors except, as he quipped, "The only doctor I like is Dr Pepper!"
His faith accompanied him to the front in France where, for thirty-nine days, he
served as a scout for his battalion. "Mostly I remember," he said, "how bad the
weather was and how we were marching from morning to night, uphill and down

hills. I remember how happy I was when I finally got back home to the farm after the war."

Moses's eldest living son said that his father has been a fiercely independent person who at 106 still cooked for himself and drove his car to church on Sundays. "He is very sharp mentally and, I might add, stubborn; he resents us trying to take care of him," Haywood said, laughing. Now, at 112, Moses argued with his nurse and asked if he could go back to his house.

It is perhaps this self-reliance, this attitude of not giving up his autonomy and free will that keeps him healthy. For Moses, however, the secret to his longevity is clear: his trust in God has given him his long life.

1895

Fannie Greenberg

Born May 24, 1895
Ottawa
Canada

"CHICKEN SCHMALTZ?" A secret of longevity? Who knew? This was the first time I had heard of this particular ingredient for a long life, but then again, this was the first Jewish supercentenarian I had photographed.

"Why does he want to take my picture?" asked 110-year-old Fannie Greenberg of the woman accompanying her, as if I wasn't standing there. "What's so special?"

"Well," I said, leaning down to her ear, " You're one of the oldest people on earth, and that's special." She shrugged off my comment and this petite woman, well under five feet, shuffled slowly on her own to an armchair in a small library at her care facility.

Fannie Greenberg's Orthodox Jewish parents lived in shtetls in Lithuania during the late 1880s. Under the harsh treatment of successive czars, Fannie's father faced a terrible choice: either be conscripted into the Russian army or endure the cruelty of the pogroms if he remained. So, traveling under the protection of a childless couple, Fannie's father left Russia under an assumed name and fled to Ottawa, Canada, for a new beginning.

Fannie grew up with five siblings in a strict kosher household. One of her earliest jobs was to clean the front of her father's general store. At the age of five she began her morning routine of sweeping the sidewalk and greeting the prime minister, Sir Wilfred Laurier, who would stride past their storefront every day on his way to work, walking in procession with his driver and horse-drawn buggy behind him for his daily constitutional.

Smart in math, Fannie was taken out of school to help in the store and she never finished high school. One of the humorous family stories passed down was of the

"Vorenden" wall. When Fannie was young and she had a problem she would go to a spot by the living room's wooden wall and talk into a special knothole. She believed her troubles would go directly to heaven for God to hear. As the story was told to me, I could visualize this little girl, her mouth pressed against the wall, whispering her troubles into a hole in the wood. A little like the Wailing Wall, this was a little girl's way of addressing her childhood dilemmas.

Surrounded by cousins and siblings living in close proximity, Fannie grew up in a nurturing network of family get-togethers and religious holidays. She lived at home, working at her family's store until she was twenty-eight when Archie Greenberg wooed her. They married and moved to Brooklyn, New York, where Fannie began the next chapter of her life as a homemaker and mother. Both her daughter and niece remember the tenement community that they lived in; like the pueblos of the early Anasazi, the apartment houses of the neighborhood were multifamily dwellings. In summer, all the windows were opened, and everyone seemed to live on the fire escapes where they communicated back and forth with one another. Everyone knew everyone else's business. Fannie's routine of life was cooking, cleaning, shopping, talking to the neighbors on the front stoop, and there was always some time for her to read the newspaper from cover to cover. Even now at 110, she receives the paper daily and reads parts of the news.

Thin and spry, Fannie said she kept kosher all her life and revealed that she never went out to eat. Food preparation was very important to her, both for health as well as for the religious ritual involved. She feels it's one of the reasons she's lived a long and healthy life. She stands by the use of chicken schmaltz, a spread of rendered chicken fat used for cooking and flavoring that would be considered lethal by today's cholesterol-conscious cooks.

Fannie's youngest brother is ninety-six today and her other siblings died in their late nineties or early one hundreds. The family members told me she was a survivor in her soul, which they likened to hardened steel that had been "tempered by the fires" of life. Maybe so, or maybe it's her DNA or her flavorful chicken soup that can be credited for her vibrant longevity.

1891

Emiliano Mercado Del Toro

Born August 21, 1891
Cabo Rojo, Puerto Rico
U.S.A.

DON EMILIANO WAS BLIND but he could see. He lay on his bed, bare-chested and frail in the midday heat. Now and again, he would raise his thin, sinewy arm to paint the air. He spoke slowly of his stories, remembering the pictures in his mind, describing the colors and the tastes from his childhood in a way that made his past come vividly alive for me. The sugar-cane fields, the family cow, the rhythms of the island, his hammock, his childhood toys, his losses and his joys were intertwined with his rich memories of his native Puerto Rico.

His family gathered around him in his room. It was bedlam in a most touching way. Don Emiliano was kissed and stroked and his hand was held by his grandnieces. With my translator repeating my questions in Spanish, Emiliano would pause, as if he were shuffling his memories, and then would answer with clarity as if the events he described had happened yesterday.

His grandfather had come from Spain in the late 1700s as a laborer. Like his grandfather and his father, Emiliano worked in the sugar-cane fields from the age of ten until well into his late eighties. As a child he would drive the ox-wagon in the fields and as he grew, he labored long hours alongside the men with his machete, first in the cane fields and later, during harvest season, in the pineapple fields of Puerto Rico.

"So what was your life like, as a child?" I asked. "I would get up and first go to our cow," Don Emiliano said. "I would squirt the milk into my mouth but, from time to time, we would not have a cow so we would climb the coconut trees for the milk to start our day. Since I was small I would go to the fields to help my father, and my mother would stay at home to do handwork like sewing sombreros from the palm leaves or do crocheting or make clothes for the family."

As a child of the late 1800s, Emiliano played with toys that he and his friends would construct using their imaginations. He described to me how they would find two bottles, push a stick into the two bottlenecks and with a string attached, pull their contraption along the ground for endless hours of entertainment.

Living under Spanish domination, Emiliano went to school through the third grade, learned to read and write Spanish, did simple mathematics, and studied some history. Emiliano recalled the events of 1898, during President McKinley's administration, when the United States occupied the island after having invaded and conquered Cuba.

"We ran for the hills, my father and I, when the troops landed at Guanica." At the age of seven, while working in the pineapple fields, Emiliano saw the Rough Riders of Teddy Roosevelt land and move north into the island. "There was no panic," he said, "Most of the people welcomed a change in the government. The Spanish were harsh.

"My days in the fields were from six to six. For that, you were paid fifty cents, but it was enough to buy some fish, some rice, and some beans. We were able to save enough to go watch Charlie Chaplin in the movie house. On Saturday night I would go out to dance, the ladies would get all dressed up, but we had no shoes.

"I never married but I had three girlfriends in my life. The first, the love of my life, was Susanne. When she died I was sad." He never had children but he cherished his sister's grandnieces, great-grandnieces, and nephews.

"He was like our grandfather," Norma, a grandniece, said. "Do you know what a rag doll is?" she asked. "He would buy these for us, give them to us, get down on the ground, and play dolls with us. He was always smiling, it was a party for us." She laughed and her voice, full of joy, trailed off. "Even our father loved him like a grandfather; I have three little children and they love him too and come here to play with him and take care of him. My daughter grabs his face and says, 'This is my nose, Grandfather.'"

Food was cooking in the kitchen; I had been invited to lunch with the family. Before we sat down to eat, I needed one last question answered. "Why," I asked, "have you been so happy?"

"Lay in a hammock," Don Emiliano responded. "It was a part of my life. At the end of a workday, I would lay in a hammock, for peace and quiet." This was his time of meditation. Maybe a cock would crow, perhaps he would hear the wind, and smell the cooking or the fires of the village as he gazed up at the sky. Surrounded by an extended family who loved him, he was able to find a personal place where he could be alone with his thoughts. In a way, Don Emiliano was like a monk who, somewhere across the planet, sat cross-legged in his own private corner, mindful of the moment.

The End

T OO OFTEN we surrender our views to the opinion professionals, the government, the managed-news information services, and managed care—without giving ourselves the opportunity and respect to do our own critical thinking and draw our own conclusions. I challenge you, the reader, to close your eyes, and for a moment try to see yourself grown old. Try to imagine the gifts you have to give, your concerns, your strengths, your weaknesses, and your impediments. Then try to imagine what you would want others to do for you, how you would want them to act toward you, how you would like someone to perceive you. Then open your eyes and do something for the elderly. Do exactly what you wanted others to do for you when you pictured yourself as old. Look into the eyes of your grandmother or grandfather and really see, perhaps for the first time, all the life experiences that shine in their eyes. Reach out to those elders you pass on the street and let them know they have been seen and heard and are not invisible. Your smile can make a difference. And what you get back will help you to live a larger, more spirited, and really fulfilling life.

Bibliography

Alberts, et al. *Molecular Biology of the Cell*. New York: Garland Publishing, 1994.

Butler, Robert N., M.D. *Being Old in America*. Baltimore: Johns Hopkins University Press, 1975

Coles, Robert. *The Moral Intelligence of Children*. New York: Random House, 1997

Elders, Joycelyn M., M.D., and David Chanoff. *Joycelyn Elders.M.D*. New York: Avon Books, 1996

Olson, Steve. *Mapping Human History*. Boston: Houghton Mifflin Company, 2002

Paster, Zorba, M.D., with Susan Meltsner. *The Longevity Code*. New York: Three Rivers Press, 2001

Perls,Thomas T., M.D., et al. *Living to 100*. New York: Basic Books, 1999

Pifer, Alan and Lydia Bronte, eds. *Our Aging Society: Paradox and Promise*. New York: W. W. Norton, 1986

Rendell-Smock, Shara. "Humour and Health." *Sideroad*, January 13, 1998

Rowe, John W., M.D., and Robert L. Kahn, Ph.D. *Successful Aging*. New York: Dell, 1999

Seligman, Martin, Ph.D. *Learned Optimism*. New York: A.A. Knopf, 1991

Snowdon, David, Ph.D. *Aging with Grace*. New York: Bantam Books, 2002

Sultanoff, Steven M., Ph.D., *Sideroad*, January 13, 1998

Vaillant, George E., M.D. *Aging Well*. New York: Little, Brown & Company, 2002

Endnotes

Dr. Elders Essay

1. He, W; Sengupta, M; Velkoff V. A., DeBarros, K. A. "65+ in the United States: 2004." Current population reports, special studies; p.23, Washington, D.C. U.S. Government Printing Office, forthcoming.

2. "Older Americans 2004: Key Indicators of Well-Being." Federal Interagency Forum on Aging-Related Statistics, http://www.agingstats.gov/chartbook2004/default.htm

3. "A Profile of Older Americans," 2003 Administration on Aging. U.S. Department of Health and Human Services, Washington, D.C.

4. Kennedy, B.P., and Kawachi, I. "Income Distribution and Mortality: Cross Sectional Ecological Study of the Robin Hood Index in the United States," *British Medical Journal*, (April 20, 1996), 1004-1007.

Photo Credits

Image of Seventh New York State Militia
  © Medford Historical Society Collection/CORBIS

Image of Child Picking Cotton
  © CORBIS

Image of Teddy Roosevelt Giving Campaign Speech
  © Bettmann/CORBIS

Image of Eleventh Cavalry Troop
  The Eleventh Cavalry troop is mounted and marching twelve abreast.
  © CORBIS

Image of Team of Horses Plowing Field
  Original caption: Wise, VA: C.E. Flory rides on a horse-drawn plow on White Farm in Virginia
  © Bettmann/CORBIS

Atomic Blast
  Collection: The Image Bank
  Photographer: Archive Holdings Inc/gettyimages

Ku Klux Klan rally, Maryland, USA (B&W)
  Collection: Stone
  Photographer: Paul Souders /gettyimages

King Edward Engine
  Collection: Hulton Archive
  Photographer: J A Hampton/gettyimages

About Earth's Elders Foundation

Earth's Elders Foundation was created to "improve the lives of the elderly by raising awareness that the elderly are valuable members of our society who are often marginalized. Earth's Elders seeks to promote respect for the aged and inspire a sense of personal responsibility that will lead to improved integration of the elderly within our society." (Earth's Elders website: www.earthselders.org)

All proceeds from this book go to the foundation, a 501(c)(3) not-for-profit corporation.